COTTISH HOUSING HANDBOOK

KW-091-972

Housing for the Disabled

Scottish Development Department
Her Majesty's Stationery Office

53704

ISBN 0 11 491583 0

CONTENTS

The Scottish Housing Handbook is intended primarily for the use of public sector housing authorities in Scotland and their consultants. The Handbook is divided for convenience into separate parts, each dealing with specific aspects of housing need and provision. In producing the complete Handbook, however, the aim has been to look at problems comprehensively to ensure that housing needs are met in the most satisfactory way.

Since housing provision is one of the elements essential to the integration of disabled people into the community this part of the Handbook should be of use to all concerned with the provision of housing for the disabled. It introduces the concept of a general provision of convenience in housing for ambulant disabled persons who form a large majority of the impaired population in Scotland, and a particular provision for the small minority who are usually wheelchair bound and who need specially designed dwellings.

The standards contained in this part replace and expand those that were previously included in the New Scottish Housing Handbook Bulletin 3: 'Housing for Old People' published in 1970. Housing for the Disabled is now discussed separately from Housing for the Elderly in view of the special needs of each group, although many old people are of course also physically handicapped.

Officers of the Scottish Development Department are available to housing authorities for consultation on any subjects covered by the Handbook.

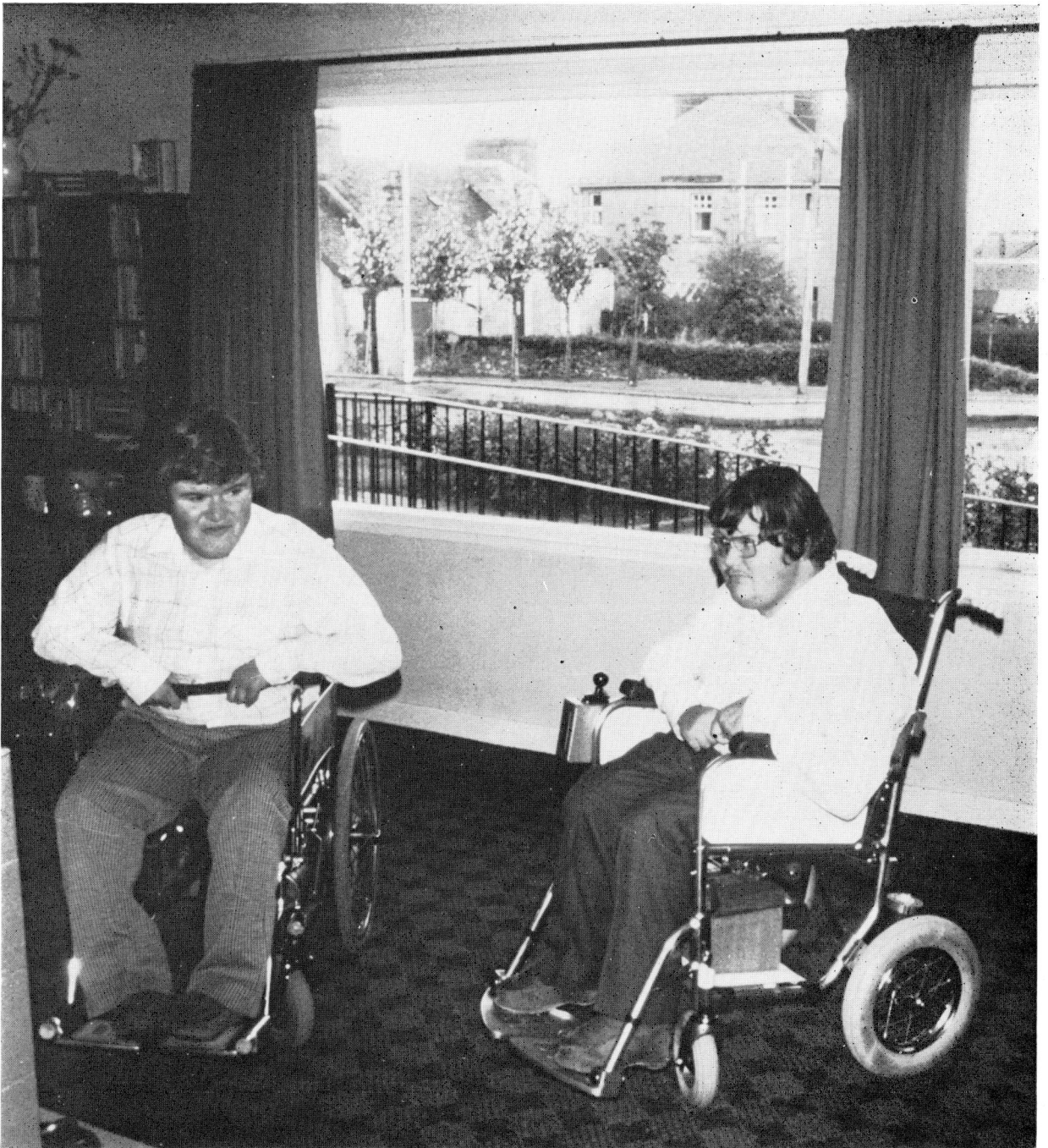

Housing for the Disabled

1.1 AIMS AND OBJECTIVES

1.1.1. The purpose of this part of the Handbook is to offer guidance on the provision of self-contained dwellings convenient for occupation by people whose physical handicap is such that they need special space or amenity standards for their dwellings in order to live as independently as possible.

1.1.2. Not all physically handicapped people require special housing as not all forms of physical impairment are equally handicapping. However, depending on the nature of the handicap, a considerable number of those who are ambulant will require suitably designed or adapted housing which would not be significantly different from mainstream housing. They are referred to throughout the Handbook as those requiring *Ambulant Disabled Housing*. They will include those who have difficulty looking after themselves or need to be helped in certain aspects of self care such as getting in and out of the house, washing, dressing, bathing and using the lavatory.

1.1.3. Some conditions, however, can result in a very severe handicap requiring the individual to be permanently in a wheelchair or needing large items of equipment. These include people who have become very severely handicapped by such conditions as multiple sclerosis, strokes, paraplegia/hemiplegia or arthritis, reducing their mobility so as to be dependent on the use of a wheelchair. Their special needs will be catered for by *Wheelchair Housing* for which design standards are given in the text.

1.1.4. It is hoped that the guidance will be adopted for private sector as well as public sector house design in order that a stock of suitable dwellings may be built up covering a wide range of house types. The recommendations are neither exhaustive nor exclusive but it is hoped that they will provide a framework for the creativity of individual designers.

1.1.5. A major contribution to the stock of dwellings suitable for disabled people is likely to come from adaptations to existing properties, and there is an important place for minor adaptations to individual dwellings in order to meet the specific needs of a known occupier. While it is not possible to make blanket recommendations to cover every situation, there are certain areas of provision where local housing authorities have a definite role to play, and further advice on adaptations is given in Section 3.

1.1.6. People with a degree of physical handicap requiring specially designed housing are of all ages and include children whose handicap makes it necessary for the family to be suitably housed to meet the child's needs. Such housing should offer a range of choice comparable to that which is available to people who are not physically handicapped.

1.1.7. Housing for the disabled is only one part of the services required by physically handicapped people and, in the assessment of need for such housing, the housing manager should consult with health and social work services. Similarly, the placing of a person in a specially designed or adapted house must be co-ordinated with the support of both statutory and voluntary services, as well as relatives and friends to ensure the essential personal care and integration of the handicapped person into the community.

1.2 DEFINITIONS

1.2.1. The following definitions are intended solely to clarify the use of these terms in this Handbook. Definitions of rooms inside the dwelling should be taken as those contained in the Scottish Building Regulations.

1.2.2. Apartment—any habitable room, excluding kitchen, bathroom, wc, utility room, storage cupboards and circulation spaces.

1.2.3. Dwelling—any self-contained place of residence including a house or flat.

1.2.4. House—a dwelling on one or more floors which is divided vertically from every other dwelling and having its principal access from ground level.

1.2.5. Flat—a dwelling on one floor, forming part of a building from some other part of which it is divided horizontally.

1.2.6. Impairment—medical condition, lacking part or all of a limb, having a defective limb, or having a defective mechanism of the body or organ which stops or limits getting about, working or self-care.

1.2.7. Physical disablement—the loss or reduction of functional physical ability, arising from impairment.

1.2.8. Handicap—the disadvantage or restriction of activity caused by physical disablement.

1.2.9. Manipulatory disablement—total or partial loss of muscle function in one or both arms or hands.

1.2.10. Sensory disablement—total or partial loss of sight, hearing, touch, smell or taste.

1.2.11. Mobility—ease of movement, ability to move around freely without physical assistance.

1.2.12. Ambulant disabled—those persons whose physical disability still permits them to walk with or without the use of walking aids, eg sticks, crutches or walking frames. This category also includes those who may occasionally make use of a wheelchair but who are not totally reliant upon it for mobility.

1.2.13. Wheelchair users—those persons whose physical disability prevents them from moving around without using a wheelchair or some other form of mechanised transport.

1.2.14. Water Closet—the term refers to the compartment and not the fitting.

1.2.15. Building Regulations—the Building Standards (Scotland) Regulations currently in force.

1.2.16. Metric Dimensions—linear dimensions on all diagrams are given in millimetres. The following abbreviations are used:

m=metres	m²=square metres
mm=millimetres	m³=cubic metres

Housing for the Disabled

2.1 SCOPE OF DOCUMENT

2.1.1. As stated in Section 1, the purpose of this part of the Handbook is to assist organisations involved with housing, public or private, towards a greater understanding and awareness of the needs of those who are disabled, so that a housing environment may be created in which they can lead as independent lives as possible.

2.1.2. While disablement may take many different forms, the handicaps imposed by physical and manipulatory disablements as opposed to sensory disablement usually have the greatest bearing on the design of housing. However, recommended design features having relevance to other forms of disability are indicated in the text, and the needs of each individual should be assessed in relation to their particular handicap.

2.1.3. Within the general context of physical disablement, the extent of care, independence, and privacy required in individual situations also varies widely. Different types of accommodation will be appropriate in each case, ranging from general needs housing at one extreme to special hospital units at the other. (See diagram on opposite page). While it is anticipated that the housing needs of the majority of the disabled will be met by ambulant disabled housing or wheelchair housing, the other forms of residential accommodation also may have a role to play.

2.1.4. Traditionally, accommodation provided for the disabled has tended to concentrate upon institutional care and new self-contained dwellings have usually been limited to one and two person houses. There is, however, a need for dwellings of all sizes to meet the requirements of disabled people living at home with their families, as well as those living on their own. The housing stock should contain a full range of suitably designed dwellings for people who are physically handicapped.

2.1.5. Fulfilment of the housing needs of disabled people encompasses a wide range of facilities, special equipment and services involving a number of different agencies, who bear financial responsibility for various different aspects. Generally, the Scottish Home and Health Department provide wheelchairs and certain other aids to mobility; Health Boards provide aids and equipment required specifically for medical and nursing purposes; Social Work Departments provide aids to daily living. The responsibility of housing authorities involves the incorporation of suitable design features, fittings and fixtures in addition to the structure of the dwellings themselves. The divisions in responsibility are particularly relevant in the context of adaptations (See 3.2.5 and Diagram).

2.1.6. The scope of this part of the Handbook therefore concentrates on the various features required in housing for people with a physical disability, and the formulation of appropriate design solutions. Generally, standard house designs may, with comparatively minor modifications linked to careful selection and location of items of equipment, be made suitable for disabled occupiers. This approach is no less valid for new housing than for conversions of existing buildings, but should in no way preclude innovation in the development of special dwelling types.

2.1.7. Many physically disabled people are also elderly; it is estimated that approximately 65% of the total impaired population are over the age of 65, but that of those described as very severely handicapped (see 2.2.10) less than 50% are over the age of 65. Attention is drawn to the Scottish Housing Handbook Part 5: 'Housing for the Elderly', in which design standards and guidance for amenity housing and sheltered housing are discussed. In situations where accommodation is to be provided for ambulant disabled elderly people, the standards appropriate to ambulant disabled housing can be applied along with either amenity housing or sheltered housing standards. Similarly, for severely disabled elderly people, it may be necessary in some cases to provide wheelchair housing incorporating old people's amenity housing or sheltered housing facilities, either as individual dwellings or within grouped schemes. (See 4.1.4.).

2.2 HOUSING NEEDS OF THE DISABLED

2.2.1. In considering housing standards and recommendations which may be suitable for general application, there is a temptation to make assumptions as to the characteristics of groups of people based entirely upon statistical averages. In the case of disabled people such assumptions are likely to be misleading because of the great variety of disabilities which have to be catered for. (See 5.1.5). It is found in practice to be inefficient and uneconomic to attempt to produce dwelling designs complete in every detail and incorporating every item of special equipment required to make the dwellings usable by all disabled people. A more realistic approach is to isolate those features which either clearly affect the majority of physical disablements and are non-specific in relation to particular conditions or are critical to the design of the basic structure of the dwelling.

2.2.2. Beyond this general level it is essential that the particular requirements of the disabled occupiers are known before specialised equipment is provided. This inevitably creates administrative difficulties if it is attempted to make allowance for these items within the normal building contract procedure, and it is usually impracticable to allocate dwellings to individuals at design stage. The tailoring of a basic dwelling design to fulfil individual needs by the addition of special fittings is thus more likely to be undertaken within the context of adaptations. (See 3.2.5, 3.3.2). The recommendations which are contained in subsequent sections of this Handbook therefore aim to cover the general requirements of disabled people up

ADMINISTRATION OF HOUSING SERVICES FOR DISABLED PEOPLE IN SCOTLAND

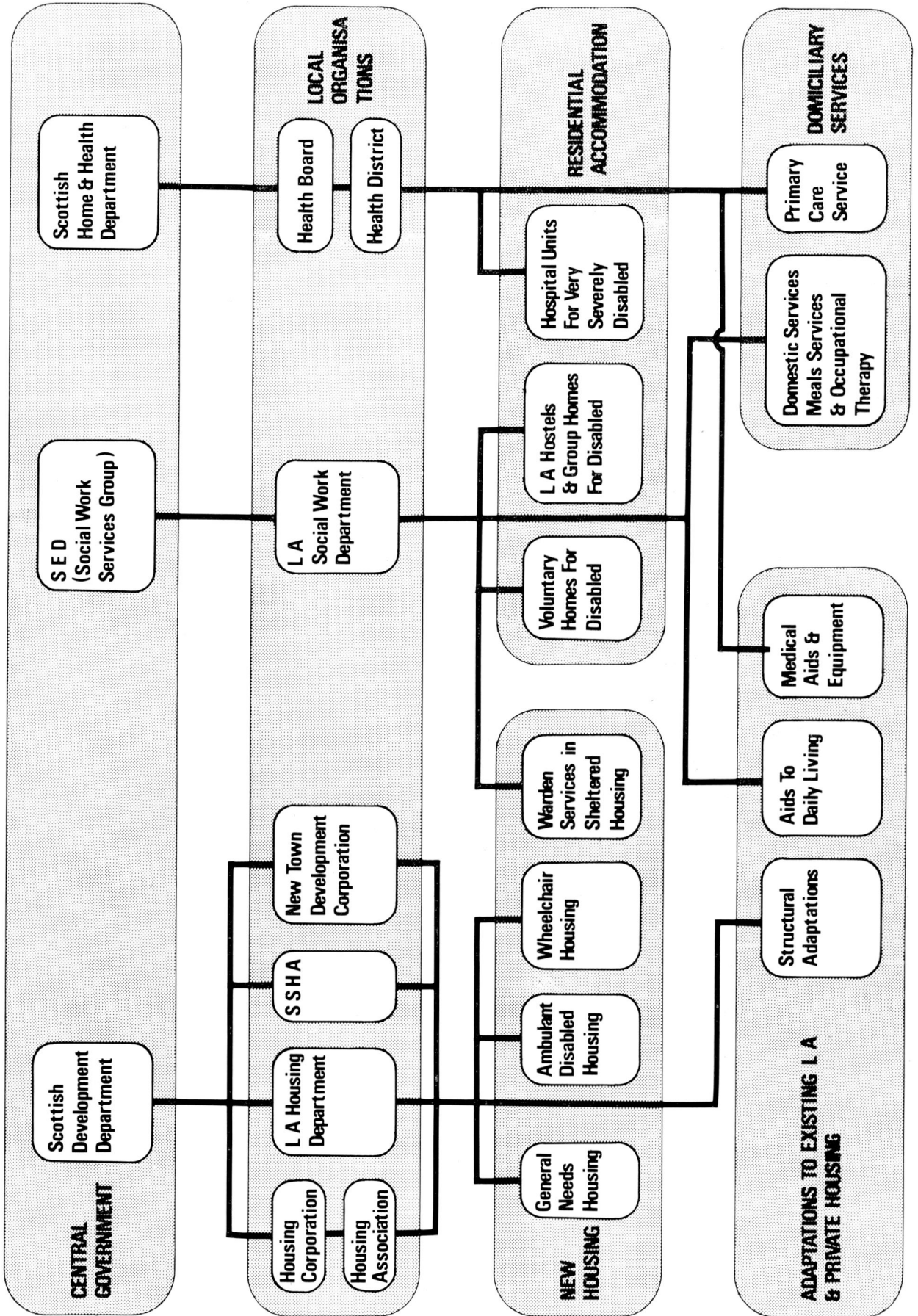

CENTRAL GOVERNMENT

- Scottish Home & Health Department
- S E D (Social Work Services Group)
- Scottish Development Department

LOCAL ORGANISATIONS

- Health Board
- Health District
- L A Social Work Department
- New Town Development Corporation
- S S H A
- L A Housing Department
- Housing Corporation
- Housing Association

RESIDENTIAL ACCOMMODATION

- Hospital Units For Very Severely Disabled
- L A Hostels & Group Homes For Disabled
- Voluntary Homes For Disabled

NEW HOUSING

- Warden Services in Sheltered Housing
- Wheelchair Housing
- Ambulant Disabled Housing
- General Needs Housing

DOMICILIARY SERVICES

- Primary Care Service
- Domestic Services Meals Services & Occupational Therapy
- Medical Aids & Equipment
- Aids To Daily Living

ADAPTATIONS TO EXISTING L A & PRIVATE HOUSING

- Structural Adaptations

Housing for the Disabled

to the point where their particular disability is likely to affect the precise specification or location of items of equipment.

2.2.3. Within the range of different types and degrees of physical disability encountered, it has already been observed (paras 1.2.12, 1.2.13), that there is an important distinction to be drawn between the ambulant disabled and wheelchair users. The significance of this distinction for house design lies in the additional space required for wheelchair manoeuvre and the need for special fittings.

2.2.4. The design guidance contained in this Handbook under the heading *Ambulant Disabled Housing* covers those basic amenities which are considered appropriate for the majority of disabled persons who may be suitably accommodated in dwellings differing only slightly from general needs housing.

2.2.5. The very small proportion of disabled people who are mainly confined to their wheelchairs would be catered for by *Wheelchair Housing*.

2.2.6. Although much of the more detailed material contained in this part of the Handbook is intended to give guidance primarily on the design of *Wheelchair Housing*, it is anticipated that, of the resources allocated to providing accommodation for disabled people, the greater proportion will be devoted to *Ambulant Disabled Housing*.

2.2.7. Provision of *Ambulant Disabled Housing* should form part of the overall housing programme of each local authority, so that a widespread stock, including adapted existing dwellings as well as new housing, is available. This will enable disabled people to remain where they are living or to be housed close to familiar surroundings and so avoid the necessity for them to move away from their friends and the area they know. It is important to avoid any sense of segregation in housing disabled people. (See 4.1.1.).

2.2.8. Furthermore, the housing requirements of individual disabled people may not remain constant as certain impairments can deteriorate quickly. In the short term housing to *Ambulant Disabled* standards may be adequate, but in the long term some disabled people may subsequently require housing designed to full *Wheelchair* standards. This emphasises the need for consultation between housing authorities and other bodies, such as health and social work with knowledge of the condition affecting the individual disabled person, and not least with the disabled people themselves and their families where possible. In particular, it may be necessary to ascertain the extent to which a severely disabled member of the family is confined to the house, their degree of ability in self-care and household chores, and the role which they expect to play within the household.

2.2.9. The exact proportion of the total population

of Scotland who are physically disabled is difficult to determine accurately and little reliance can be placed on estimates of actual numbers of disabled people because of inconsistencies in the methods of classifying different types or degrees of disability. However, the estimated proportions of the various categories in the disabled population are included below as percentages in order to present at least some idea of the overall scale of the problem at national level.

2.2.10. From information contained in the 1968-69 Office of Population Censuses and Surveys (OPCS) Survey, 'Handicapped and Impaired in Great Britain' published in 1971, which was not comprehensive but is the principal source of statistical information on this subject, it is estimated that approximately 6% of the total population of Scotland have some form of physical or sensory impairment. These can be divided into four main categories as follows:

a. 61% have negligible or minor impairments and can live normal independent lives, and many of these would have no special housing need.

b. 21% have appreciable impairments but are able to get out and around on their own.

c. 12% are severely impaired and may occasionally use a wheelchair but many of these are still ambulant and can get out and around if accompanied or using a walking-aid.

d. 6% are very severely impaired, they frequently require a wheelchair to move around, many are either wheelchair-bound or bedfast and some of this group will be in need of constant care or special medical facilities.

2.2.11. Thus about half of those in category d. and a quarter of those in category c. would be regular wheelchair users for whom wheelchair housing would be appropriate ie 6% of the impaired population or 0·36% of the total population of Scotland. The average household is less than three persons, and if it is assumed that there is usually no more than one disabled person in each household then the amount of wheelchair housing which will eventually be required is unlikely to exceed even 1% of the total housing stock.

2.2.12. Of the remainder of the impaired population, 30% from category a. can be housed satisfactorily in mainstream dwellings and 3% from category d. are so disabled as to require constant care in appropriate units, leaving 61%, or 3·6% of the total population of Scotland, for whom ambulant disabled housing would be appropriate. By the same calculation as that for wheelchair housing, the number of dwellings which will be required to be designed to ambulant disabled housing standards is approximately 10% of the total housing stock.

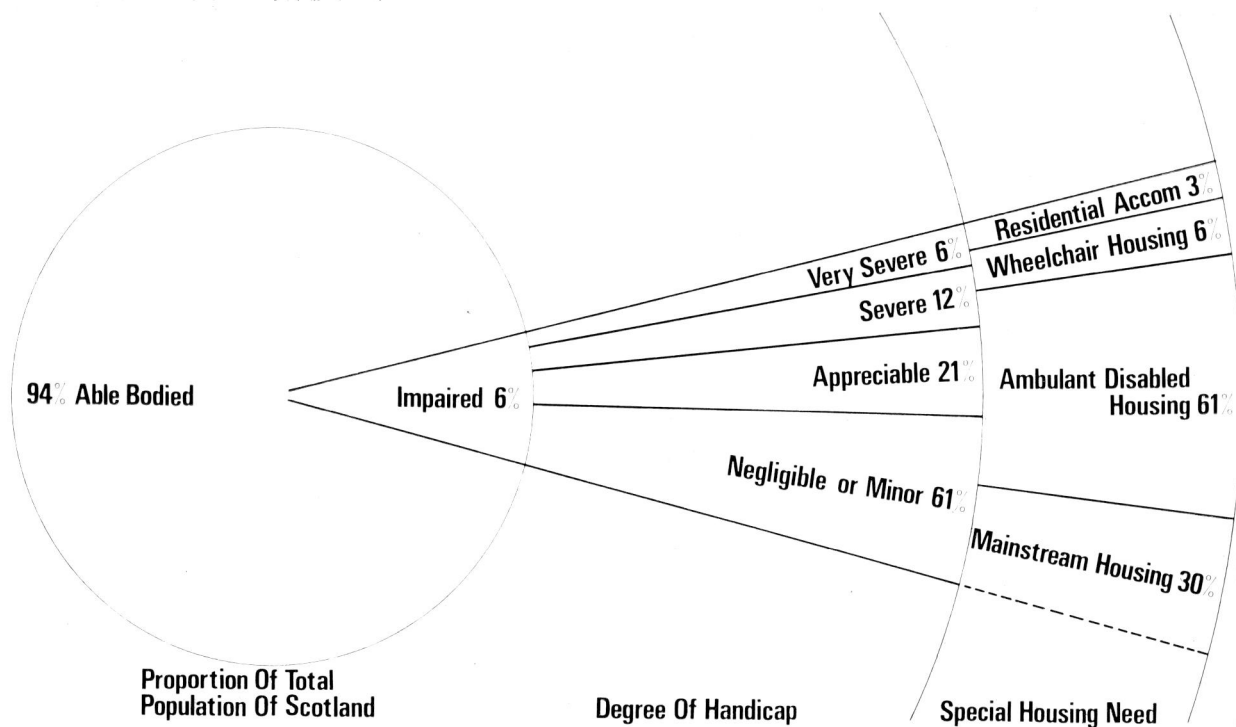

94% Able Bodied

Impaired 6%

Very Severe 6%

Severe 12%

Appreciable 21%

Negligible or Minor 61%

Residential Accom 3%

Wheelchair Housing 6%

Ambulant Disabled Housing 61%

Mainstream Housing 30%

Proportion Of Total Population Of Scotland

Degree Of Handicap

Special Housing Need

PROPORTIONS OF IMPAIRED POPULATION (OPCS 1971)

2.2.13. These figures, however, only give an indication of the long term national requirement and do not refer to specific local situations where a lack of suitable dwellings may indicate a need for larger proportions of ambulant disabled housing or wheelchair housing in actual construction programmes. For mainly topographical reasons it would not be practicable to provide all new ground floor dwellings to ambulant disabled standards but it is hoped that the shortfall in this type of housing will be overcome by a greater emphasis on adaptations to the existing stock.

2.2.14. Whereas the OPCS survey and the conclusions reached above give broad indications of the likely scale of requirement, it is essential that each housing authority should provide for the needs of disabled people within their particular area and it may sometimes be necessary to carry out local surveys. For instance, a survey carried out in SE Scotland in 1975 on children handicapped with spinabifida indicated that approximately 75% were living in unsuitable accommodation. Local authorities should, of course, take the needs of the disabled into account in their overall assessment of local housing needs, which is discussed more fully in the Scottish Housing Handbook, Part 1: 'Assessing Housing Needs—A Manual of Guidance'. Assessment of housing needs should also take account of population trends, particularly with regard to the increasing numbers of severely disabled people who are surviving into old age, for instance as the result of improvements in the

treatment of spinal injuries. (See 2.1.7.). The Housing Authority should seek to draw on data held by social work departments, Health Boards, and any voluntary organisations who provide services for handicapped people, and they should consider adaptations to existing dwellings, as well as new provision, in drawing up their building programmes.

2.3 ADMINISTRATIVE CONSIDERATIONS

2.3.1. Local housing authorities have a statutory duty under their general housing powers to consider the housing conditions in their district and the needs of the district with respect to the provision of further housing accommodation. This extends to meeting the requirements of special groups, including the disabled.

2.3.2. In certain circumstances purpose built housing will be unnecessary when the needs of a disabled occupier can be met by adaptation of an existing house. Such adaptations should only be carried out after consultation with the social work and health personnel who will be acquainted with the needs of the disabled person's household as well as the limitations of the individual's handicap. (See 5.1.7.).

2.3.3. Social work authorities have statutory powers to enable them to contribute towards the cost of adapting houses to meet the needs of the disabled in both the public and private housing spheres.

2.3.4. In deciding on their policy for providing houses suitable for disabled people, local authorities will require to co-ordinate their building proposals with the adaptation of their existing housing stock, and with other schemes for rehabilitation of buildings and general improvement.

2.3.5. Registered housing associations have a role to play in the provision of housing for the disabled either by including a proportion of suitable dwellings within schemes designed predominantly for general needs, or by establishing grouped sheltered housing or, for cases of special need, by providing hostel accommodation. Local authorities should take into account the contribution which housing associations may make to the stock of suitable dwellings when assessing needs of the disabled within their area.

BIBLIOGRAPHY

2.1 *Towards a Housing Policy for Disabled People: Report of the Working Party on Housing for Disabled People*, Central Council for the Disabled, London 1976.

2.1 *Report of the Working Party on Housing for Disabled People*, Scottish Committee for the Welfare of the Disabled, Edinburgh 1974.

2.1 *Housing and Social Work, A Joint Approach: The Report of the Morris Committee on Links between Housing and Social Work*, SDD, HMSO 1975.

2.1 *Scottish Housing Handbook, Part 5: Housing for the Elderly*, SDD, HMSO.

2.2 *Handicapped and Impaired in Great Britain, Part 1*, Harris with Cox and Smith, Office of Population Censuses and Surveys, HMSO 1971.

2.2 *Handicapped and Impaired in Great Britain, Part 2: Work and Housing of Impaired Persons in Great Britain*, Buckle, OPCS, HMSO 1971.

2.2 *Scottish Social Work Statistics*, Scottish Office, HMSO 1974.

2.2 *Social Implications of Spina Bifida—A Study in South-East Scotland*, Woodburn, National Federation for Educational Research 1975.

2.2 *Housing Needs and Resources*, SDD Circular No 50/1975.

2.2 *Housing Needs and Strategies*, SDD Circular No 100/1975

2.2 *Assessment of Housing Needs*, SDD Circular No 14/1976.

2.2 *Scottish Housing Handbook, Part 1: Assessing Housing Need*, SDD, HMSO 1977.

2.2 *Preparation of Housing Plans 1977*, SDD Circular No 6/77.

2.3 *Chronically Sick and Disabled Persons Act, 1970*, HMSO, (and as extended by the *Chronically Sick and Disabled Persons (Scotland) Act, 1972*, HMSO).

2.3 *Housing (Scotland) Act 1974*, HMSO.

2.3 *Housing for People who are Physically Handicapped*, DOE Circular No 74/1974 Welsh Office Circular No 120/1974.

2.3 *Housing for Physically Handicapped People*, SDD Circular No 61/1975.

2.3 *Housing (Scotland) Act 1974: Housing Corporation, Housing Associations and Housing Authorities in Scotland*, SDD Circular No 10/1975.

3.0 Adaptations

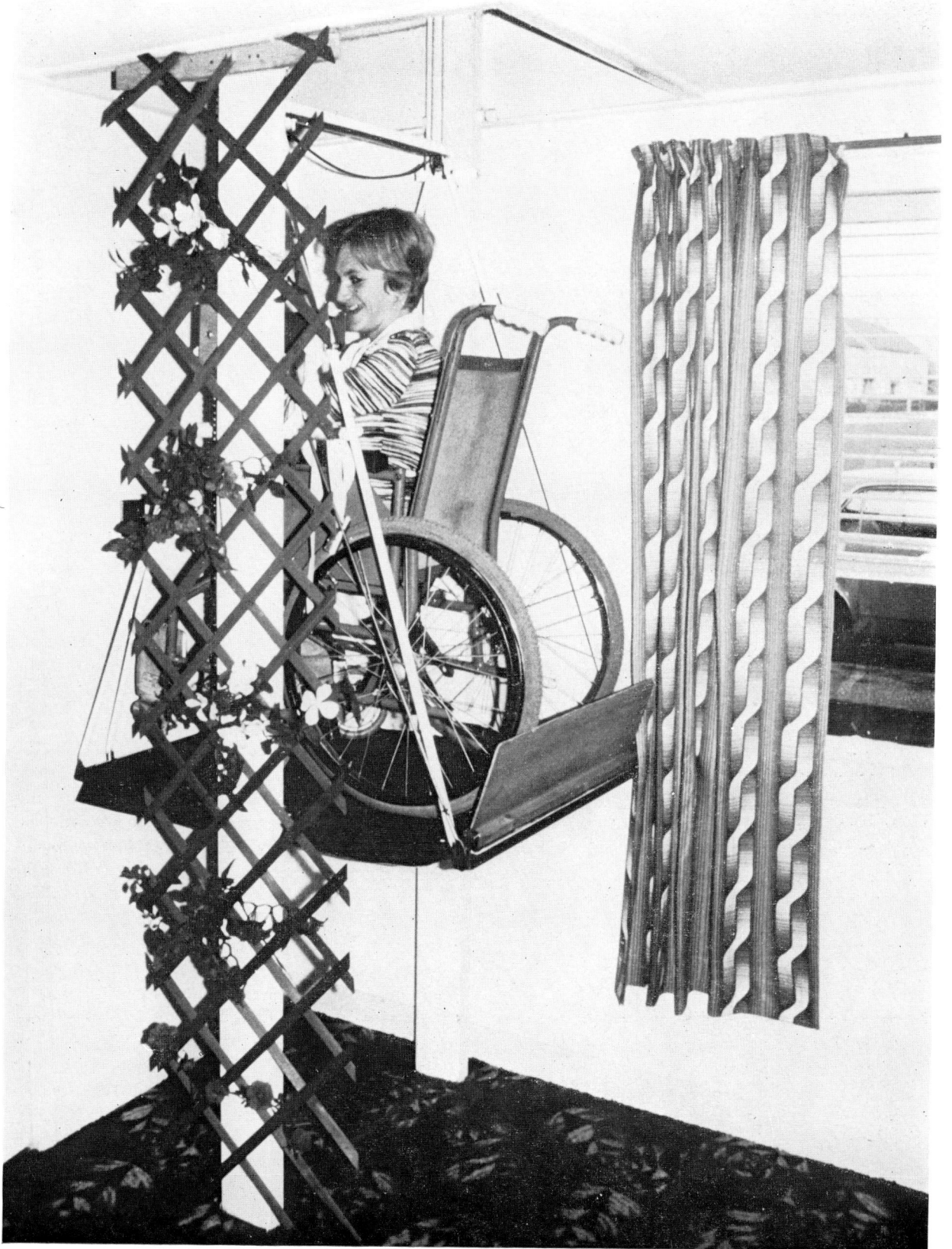

3.1 PRIMARY CONSIDERATIONS

3.1.1. One of the most important aspects of the provision of housing for the disabled, which commends itself on social as well as economic grounds involves the adaptation of existing dwellings. Adaptations, unrelated to other building work, will be necessary in order to cater for specific instances of need, although they may also sometimes occur as part of general improvement work particularly in situations where stress is laid upon the contribution which building rehabilitation may make towards meeting general housing needs.

3.1.2. An important advantage of this type of provision is that it will maintain the familiar environment of place, friends and neighbours. To continue to be part of an established community is of importance especially for elderly disabled people for whom removal to a new place may give rise to social isolation and loneliness. (See 4.1.1, 4.1.2). Co-operation between local authority housing and social work departments is essential in establishing areas of need, in locating dwellings suitable for conversion and in the allocation of the completed dwellings once they have been adapted to appropriate tenants. Proximity to communal services and facilities such as shops, doctors' surgeries, post offices, etc must also be considered when assessing needs and proposing solutions. (See 4.2.4).

3.1.3. Where disabled people already occupy inappropriate dwellings, adaptations may not always be practicable for a variety of reasons. In such cases the only alternative may be for the occupier to consider moving to more suitable new or existing housing.

3.1.4. Even relatively inexpensive adaptations to existing houses may prove to be beyond the means of

Wheelchair lift between livingroom and bedroom in 2-storey house with awkward stair.

the occupier and social work authorities have powers to pay a proportion of the cost, or the full cost, of alterations to any house whether in the public or private sector to make it more suitable for occupation by a handicapped person. In the case of adaptation by a housing authority of a house held on its housing revenue account the expenditure involved (with the exception of any contribution made by the social work authority) will be a proper charge to the housing revenue account.

3.1.5. Housing authorities may wish to consider taking the opportunity, during the implementation of improvement programmes, of adapting some houses to make them suitable for occupation by disabled people.

3.1.6. The adaptations might be related specifically to the identified needs of particular disabled people or, if no detailed assessment of needs had been made, might take the form of relatively minor works to make a number of houses potentially suitable before further specific adaptation.

3.2 REQUIREMENTS OF THE INDIVIDUAL

3.2.1. Any attempt to make recommendations for adaptations of existing housing to meet the needs of disabled persons has to recognise that the nature of the requirement may vary widely according to disabilities of the individual occupier. It is clear that within the confines of their disablement a person may become accustomed to the limitations of his own dwelling environment in much the same way as any other occupier. Of particular significance in this context is the extent to which the handicapped can rely and call upon relatives, friends or neighbours for assistance, and the degree of dependence upon the co-operation of local delivery services and social services.

3.2.2. The ability to cope with a particular situation also depends greatly on the type and extent of a person's handicap, motivation, degree of frailty, and the type of equipment or aids required to achieve mobility within the dwelling. The requirements of any individual occupier are likely to change over a period of time due to advancing age or deterioration of their medical condition. It has been found convenient elsewhere (see 2.2.4, 2.2.5) to give separate recommendations for the majority who are partially disabled and usually ambulant and the minority who are severely disabled many of whom are wheelchair bound. This distinction is significant in relation to space standards and to the type of amenities and location of certain fittings. However it should be remembered that there is considerable overlapping between the various categories of disablement in the extent of a disability and capabilities of the individual. For example wheelchair users are frequently better at coping with household chores than some of the ambulant who use walking aids. Nevertheless an important factor in specific as

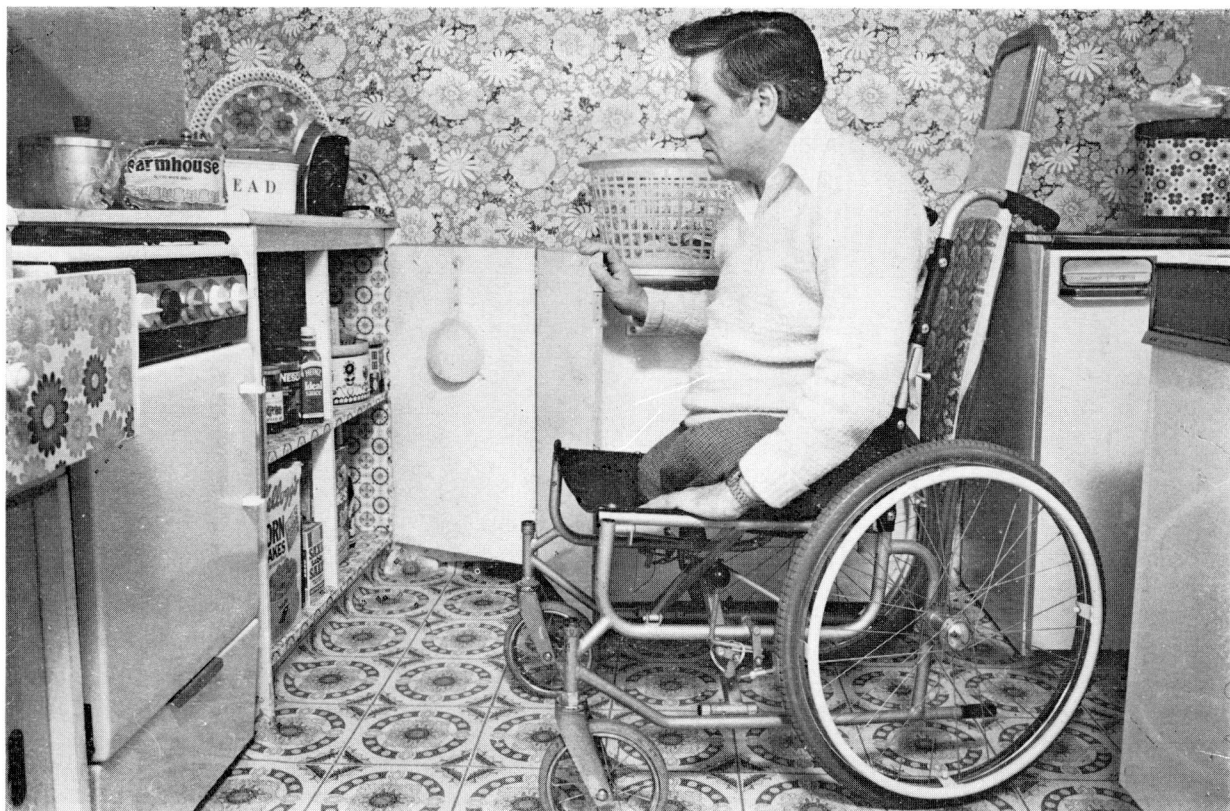

Simple but effective adaptation carried out by disabled tenant. Access to cupboard is facilitated by hingeing doors together so that they fold out of the way when open.

opposed to general adaptations is that the disability of the tenant is known and the adaptation can be tailored to the needs of an individual person rather than an amorphous group.

3.2.3. Two main factors govern the need for adaptations apart from social factors, firstly the nature of the person's disability and secondly the physical character of the accommodation. It is therefore difficult to classify types of requirement according to disabilities, although there are clearly some design factors which are common to a variety of situations. These include width of doorways, type of door and window ironmongery, location of power points and light switches, width of hall, arrangements of kitchen and accessibility of storage, size of bathroom, location of fittings and heating comfort levels.

3.2.4. Bearing in mind the need for distinction in space standards some additional amenities may be incorporated covering a variety of options. These might range from such items as adjustable storage units and grab rails to special hoists and ceiling tracks for particular severely disabled people, but for clinical as well as economic reasons it is essential for the specific circumstances of a prospective severely disabled occupier to be made known to the housing authority before expensive adaptations are carried out and equipment is installed. Ideally it should be possible for further alterations or additions to the dwelling structure to be made at a later date as user needs change.

3.2.5. It is essential that local authority housing

departments and social work departments should co-operate with health boards in order to ensure that appropriate house adaptations are carried out, that suitable equipment is installed where required, within the shortest possible time for the convenience of the disabled person. Prompt completion of the work is essential if the maximum benefit is to be gained from any housing proposals for adaptations and careful control is necessary. Any delay through lack of co-ordination between the various bodies concerned can only serve to exacerbate the problem of particular disabled occupiers and in some cases could lead to permanent serious deterioration in the occupier's physical condition.

3.3 SUITABILITY OF EXISTING STOCK

3.3.1. In the case of adaptations to existing dwellings, the particular disability will frequently be known and designed for, but sometimes the local authority may wish to anticipate needs in their housing programmes and prepare accommodation that is convenient for the disabled. In selecting such dwellings for adaptations from the existing stock, it is desirable to choose those types which already contain some of the required features, particularly with regard to level or ramped approach and access, room sizes and circulation space, and which appear to be capable of conversion at reasonable cost.

3.3.2. Particular amenities to suit the degree of disability will invariably be needed above the basic provision, and a selected choice of solutions which can be tailored to suit the requirements of a specific disabled person will be advantageous. The existing house

Stair-lift, folded against wall when not in operation; with seat back and footrest unfolded; ready for use.

arrangement or accommodation size does not necessarily have to be retained as many larger houses are often under-occupied.

3.3.3. In a study commissioned by SDD in 1974 and carried out by the Scottish Local Authorities Special Housing Group, a sample of local authority tenants dependent for mobility on walking aids or wheelchairs was identified and a survey carried out of existing house amenities and any adaptations made to render the dwelling more convenient for disabled people. A representative selection of ground floor flats in local authority housing built between the two World Wars potentially suitable for convenient occupation by disabled persons was chosen and recommendations regarding special facilities needed to enable typical ground floor accommodation to be made suitable for disabled people were called for. The study was concerned with the dwelling structure rather than the degree and types of disability, and this, together with the small number of examples of such dwellings, made it impossible for any statistically reliable conclusions to be drawn. Nevertheless, the study confirmed that many of the disabled are elderly, and live alone or in 2 person households mostly in dwellings unsuited to their disablement and often too large for their comfort or particular needs. Extensive and costly adaptation to the majority of houses surveyed was not advocated as it was argued that with a reasonable stock of Scottish inter-war ground floor accommodation related to the probable numbers required there was sufficient margin of choice available for selection purposes which was capable of suitable conversion at reasonable cost.

3.4 STANDARDS FOR ADAPTATIONS

3.4.1. Social work authorities and housing authorities will have built up sufficient information based on experience to cope with most minor adaptation requirements. Where the anticipated life of the property is 30 years or more, major conversions will be expected to conform broadly with the standards for new building, detailed in sections 4 and 5 and summarised in Section 6, although full compliance with them may not be practicable. Overall costs should be reasonable in relation to the expected life of the building especially where adaptations are contemplated for dwellings expected to have a comparatively short life.

3.4.2. In any comprehensive assessment of local housing needs, and in the consequent formulation of policies to meet those needs, it follows that careful evaluation of the existing stock and its potential will play an important part. The identification therefore of the housing conditions of disabled people, and the potential improvement which the existing stock, through adaptation, can offer, will be an essential part of this process. (See Scottish Housing Handbook, Part 1: 'Assessing Housing Need').

BIBLIOGRAPHY

3.1 *Housing (Scotland) Act 1974: Requirements to be met by Houses Improved with the Aid of Grant*, SDD Circular No 72/1975

3.2 *The Elderly and the Disabled in Rehabilitated Housing: Guidance for General Housing Associations*, National Building Agency, London 1977

3.2 *Made to Measure: Domestic Extensions and Adaptations for Handicapped Persons*, Cheshire County Council Department of Architecture, 1973

3.2 *Three Wheelchair Units: A J Handbook of Housing Rehabilitation*, Section 3, Case Study 3, Architects' Journal 30 April 1977

3.3 *Disabled Tenants and the Older Housing Stock*, Scottish Local Authorities Special Housing Group, 1975 (Commissioned by SDD, available to SLASH members only).

Housing for the Disabled

4.1 GROUPING OF DWELLINGS

4.1.1. In increasing the independence of disabled people through the provision of suitably designed self-contained accommodation, it is necessary to avoid concentrating the dwellings in large distinct groups. Exceptionally, there may be a local need to provide housing in groups where there is possibility of encouraging mutual support between handicapped people or where there is a need to provide greater support than would be possible with dispersed housing, but it is preferable for disabled people's housing to be integrated with general needs housing either singly or in small groups of dwellings. The most suitable form of accommodation would be in single-storey detached, semi-detached or terraced houses, ground floor flats, and in certain circumstances two-storey houses or flats at upper levels served by lifts. (See 1.2.3-5, 4.4.8-10, 5.3.8).

4.1.2. An important psychological factor is the significant role which able-bodied neighbours may play

in the creation of an environment where disabled persons can live safely in their own dwellings. Severely disabled people may also rely on help from friends and relatives for some aspects of housekeeping, especially shopping. The most important consideration, however, is the sense of security which the disabled occupier may have in the knowledge that there is someone close at hand to assist in an emergency. (See 1.1.7 and 5.9.5).

4.1.3. For very severely disabled people confined to their dwellings or unable to venture far unassisted, an opportunity to see the activities of the outside world and to communicate with it is an essential ingredient of integration. This factor emphasises the need for disabled people's housing to be grouped among or beside general needs housing. (See 5.4.4).

4.1.4. In a few exceptional circumstances it may be desirable for dwellings for disabled people to be incorporated in sheltered housing schemes, where assistance from neighbours can be supplemented by the presence of a warden. Dwellings in this type of scheme are often grouped together and sometimes linked to communal facilities. However, in most cases a more dispersed type of provision would be appropriate, with individual 'sheltered' dwellings set among a layout of general needs housing. (As in 4.1.1). These dwellings would be linked to a call system connecting to a warden's house or to an existing nearby sheltered housing scheme.

4.1.5. General guidance for the layout of housing areas, grouping of dwellings and the design of external

Examples of dwellings designed for special needs arranged singly or in small groups among schemes of predominantly mainstream housing.

Small group of dwellings for disabled people close to centre of village and linked by alarm call to nearby nursing home. Gently sloping paths and ramps to entrance doors.

spaces is contained in Scottish Housing Handbook, Part 3: 'Housing Development: Layout, Roads and Services'.

4.2 LOCATION OF DEVELOPMENTS

4.2.1. Sites for self-contained dwellings for the disabled should be chosen within easy reach of local facilities such as shops, church, public house, post office, surgery, etc accessible by level or gently sloping pedestrian routes. (See 4.3.5). Family dwellings should also be within easy reach of play areas which could also incorporate some equipment suitably designed for use by disabled children.

4.2.2. Housing Authorities should consider the location of dwellings in relation to suitable sources of employment for disabled people and to community facilities.

4.2.3. Wherever possible, all dwellings for the disabled should have easy access to public transport, and should be close to a bus stop. Access to railway stations should also be considered, particularly in urban situations.

4.2.4. All concerned with planning housing for disabled people should consider its location in relation to public buildings which provide suitable facilities such as lifts, escalators, ramps and handrails on access and circulation routes. This applies to provisions in community facilities generally, as required by the Chronically Sick and Disabled Persons Act. Under this Act, public access routes and buildings containing suitable facilities for wheelchair users are required to be clearly identified by sign-posting systems incor-

Sheltered housing schemes often contain some dwellings designed for use by elderly disabled people.

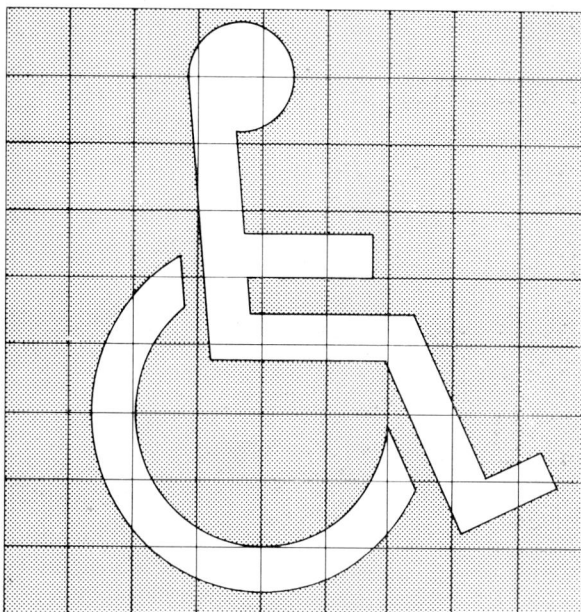

porating the standard international symbol of access. If necessary, designers should draw the attention of responsible authorities to what is needed.

4.2.5. In situations where there is an established infrastructure of residential roads, for instance in small scale infill schemes or urban redevelopments, selection of sites will be directly affected by the suitability of existing access routes in terms of slope. (See 3.3.2.). Selection of appropriate locations within completely new areas of housing may not always be so straightforward, but even on some steeply sloping sites, acceptable gradients for approach roads and footpaths may be achieved by careful use of the contours in planning the layout. This would also minimise the additional cost of underbuilding and site works required to provide level or ramped access to both sides of houses (see 4.6.2.), or split level access to flats. (See 4.4.10.). It is therefore recommended that as a general rule housing for the disabled should be located on sites which are reasonably level or with slopes not exceeding 1:12, and preferably nearer 1:20.

4.3 APPROACH AND ACCESS TO DWELLINGS

4.3.1. Provided that the layout of roads in housing areas conforms to the recommendations in Scottish Housing Handbook, Part 3: 'Housing Development: Layout, Roads and Services' the requirements of disabled people will not generally affect the design of the roads themselves except insofar as they are associated with pedestrian routes likely to be used by disabled people.

4.3.2. One of the major problems encountered by disabled people in daily living stems from difficulty in crossing the road to gain access to shops and local centres. (See 4.2.4.). Therefore, at pedestrian crossings, roadway camber or crossfall/gradients should not exceed 1:20. At pedestrian crossings, entrances to driveways and at street corners, road and pavement levels should be blended by lowering the kerb to a level not exceeding 25mm above the adjacent roadway. Dishing or ramping of the pavement should have a gradient not steeper than 1:6 nor longer than 1200mm. It is desirable that at pedestrian crossings controlled

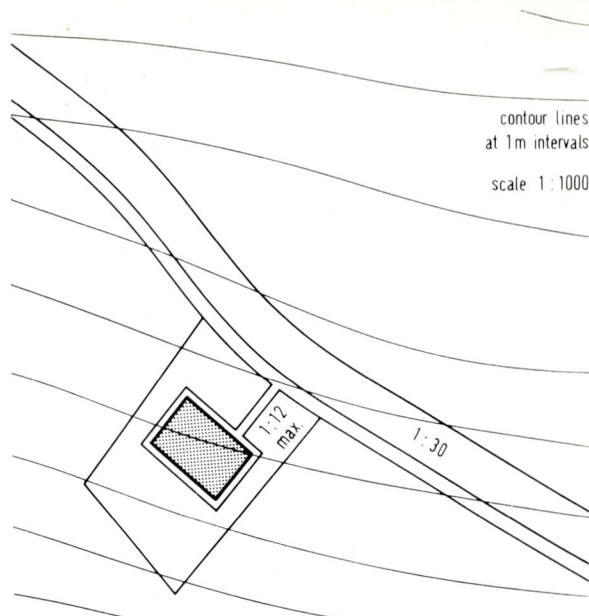

contour lines at 1m intervals

scale 1 : 1000

by traffic lights, both visual and audible warning devices should be provided and in areas of heavy traffic, crossings and road junctions should be adequately illuminated.

4.3.3. Pavements or footpaths should be 1800mm wide but this may be reduced to 1200mm where the footpath serves no more than two dwellings. Pavements and footpaths should be crowned or laid to a crossfall not steeper than 1:100 to permit rain-water run-off. Excessive pavement camber can be awkward for wheelchair users who continually have to correct the direction of movement of the wheelchair to counter the bias induced by the crossfall.

4.3.4. Obstructions should be avoided where possible and the design and location of lamp posts, signs, post boxes, manhole-covers and gratings should be carefully considered, particularly where the route may be used by visually handicapped people. Slotted gratings should be arranged with the bars running at right angles to the direction of travel. Surfacing should be firm and even; loose gravel, cobbles or setts should be avoided. Pavings to ramped surfaces must be laid

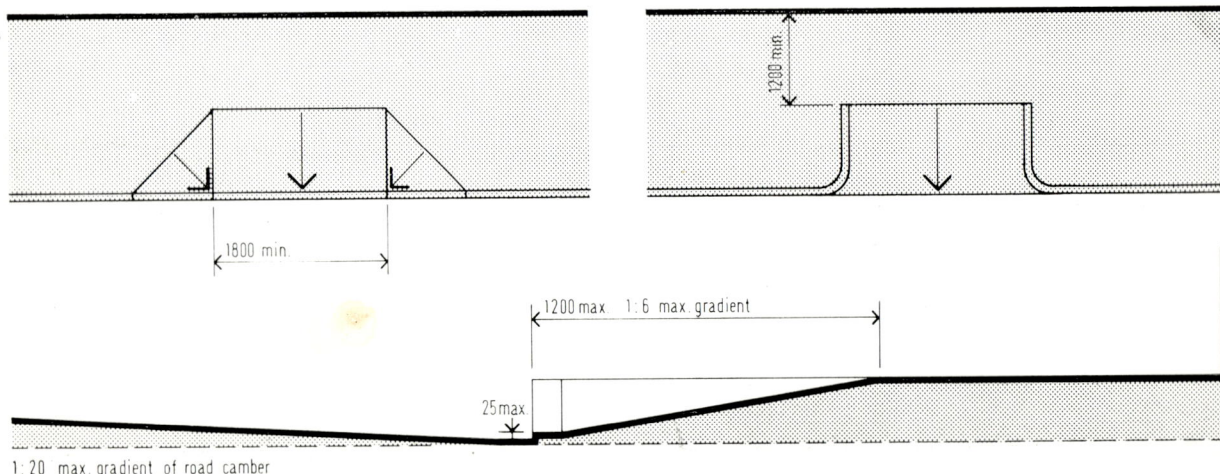

1800 min.

1200 min.

1200 max. 1:6 max. gradient

25 max

1:20 max. gradient of road camber

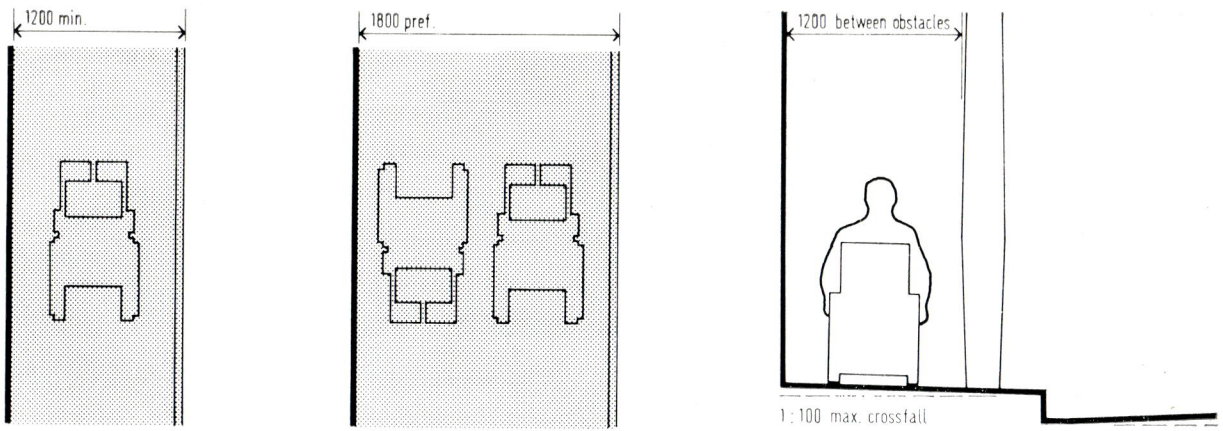

1200 min.   1800 pref.   1200 between obstacles

1:100 max. crossfall

with flush joints and incorporate a non-slip finish or texture. The use of materials having a distinctive texture greatly assists in guiding those who are visually handicapped, in indicating approach to changes in level or direction, and the proximity of hazards or obstructions.

4.3.5. Footpaths may have a continuous slope of unrestricted length provided that the gradient is no more than 1:30. For gradients between 1:30 and 1:20 level rest areas are required at 18m intervals. For ramps with gradients between 1:20 and 1:12 level rest areas are required at 9m intervals. Ramps giving access to disabled people's dwellings should generally be no steeper than 1:12 and a gradient nearer 1:20 is preferred.

4.3.6. Slopes steeper than 1:12 are possible provided that they are severely restricted in length. For gradients between 1:12 and 1:8, maximum length should be 2400mm. For gradients between 1:8 and 1:6, maximum length should be 1200mm. Ramps at these steeper gradients may be necessary in some special circumstances, for instance in adapting a house where space at the entrance is very limited, but it would be essential to establish in advance that the particular wheelchair user was capable of negotiating the slope.

4.3.7. Level landings for wheelchairs at least 1200mm long must be provided at the head, foot and any changes in direction of the ramp, although these may be included in any adjoining area of level paving. Where a landing at the head of a ramp occurs immediately outside the entrance door to the dwelling, it is desirable that some protection from the weather is provided.

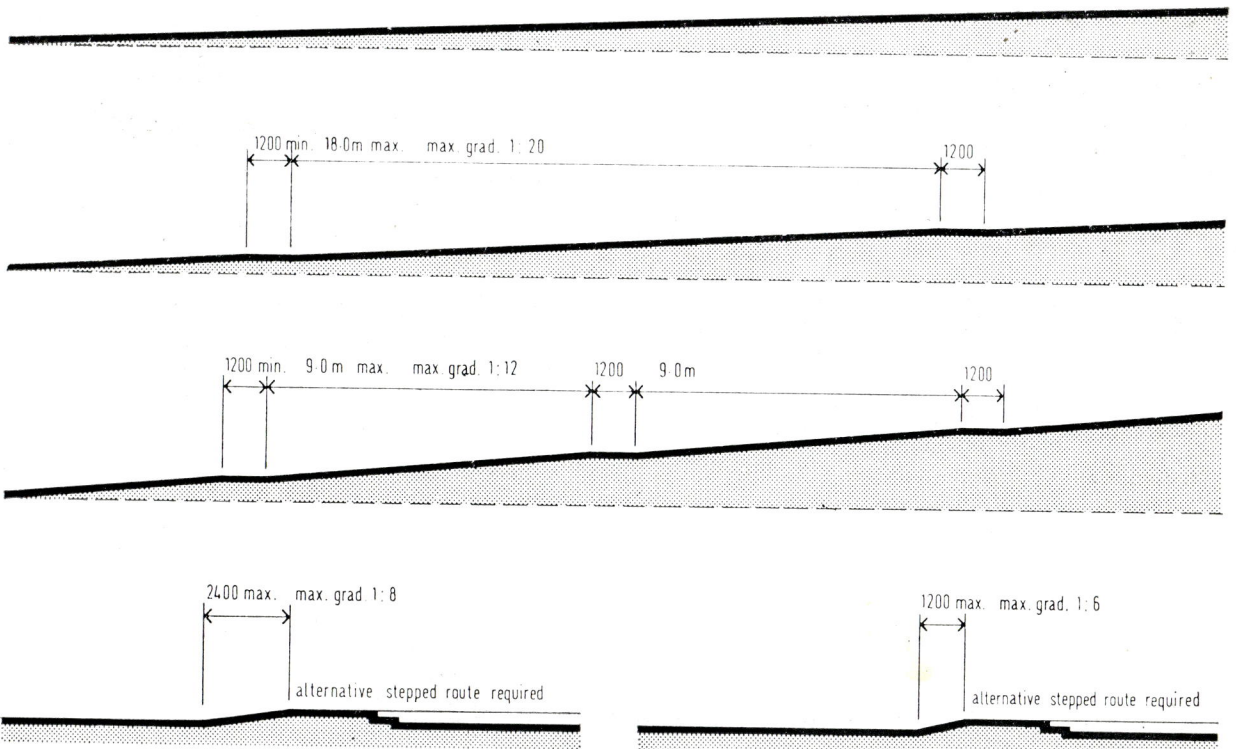

1:30 max. gradient continuous slope of unlimited length

1200 min. 18.0m max. max. grad. 1:20   1200

1200 min. 9.0m max. max. grad. 1:12   1200   9.0m   1200

2400 max. max. grad. 1:8 — alternative stepped route required   1200 max. max. grad. 1:6 — alternative stepped route required

Housing for the Disabled

4.3.8. Handrails should be provided where either the ramp is steeper than 1:20 or there is a drop of more than 600mm to the side. A 50mm high kerb should also be provided for safety purposes at exposed edges. The handrail should generally be set at a height of 950mm above the ramp surface and should extend for at least 300mm beyond the ends of the ramp. A lower handrail at about 750mm may be preferred by some people and in some cases ramps can be constructed with handrails at both heights to cater for a variety of users. Handrails may also be used to guide the blind along tortuous routes or to indicate entrances to buildings.

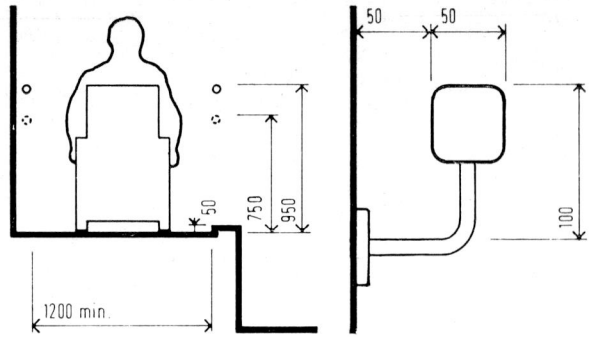

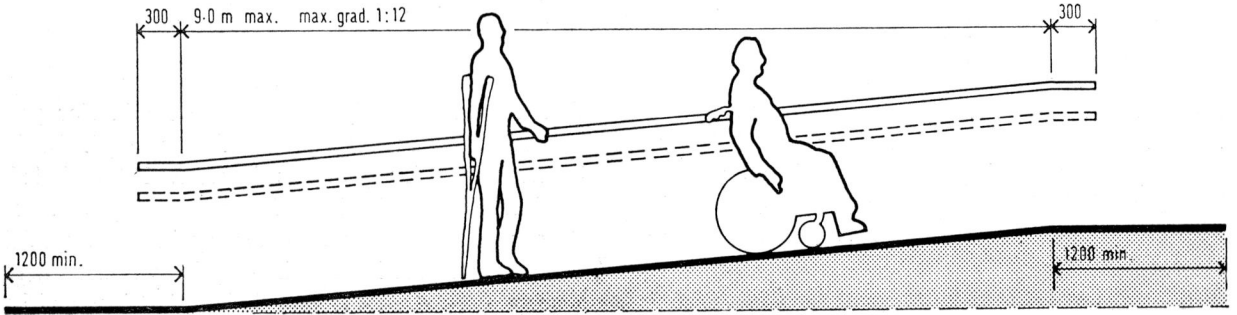

4.3.9. Small changes in level and single steps should be avoided in approach routes, with ramps substituted if necessary. However, where it is not possible to provide ramps to a suitable gradient of 1:12 or shallower, an alternative stepped access route should be provided for use by the able-bodied and ambulant disabled, for whom negotiation of such a slope could be hazardous. The suggested height for risers is 140mm and width of treads 380mm. Dwellings designed specifically for use by ambulant and semi-ambulant disabled people may have a wide shallow step at the entrance in place of a ramp. Care needs to be taken when making this provision as its installation prevents access for visiting purposes by disabled friends who may be confined to wheelchairs, unless assistance is available or a removable ramp is provided. The tread should be 400-600mm to facilitate use of walking-aids.

4.3.10. Although suspended timber floors are the traditional method of constructing ground floors in Scotland, in housing for the disabled consideration should be given to using solid concrete floors as it is thereby possible to avoid a large change in level at the entrance door. There may be cost savings as well as some functional advantages to be gained by this form of construction.

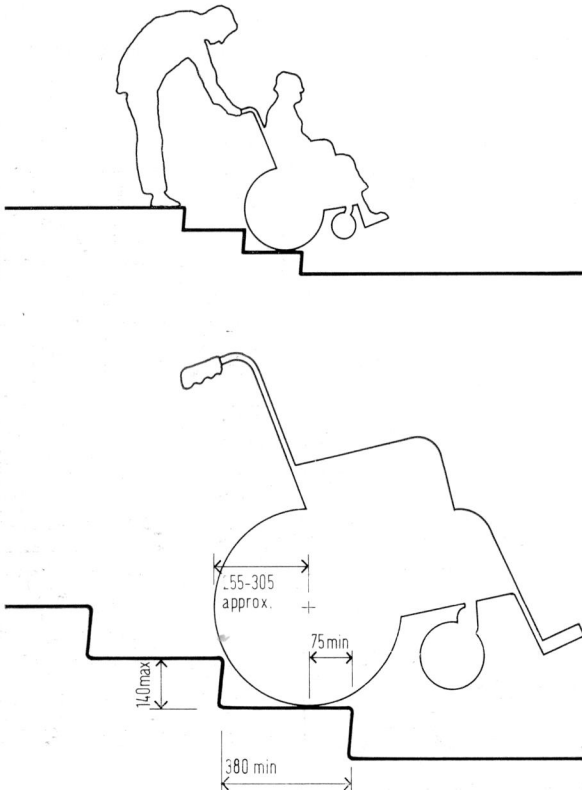

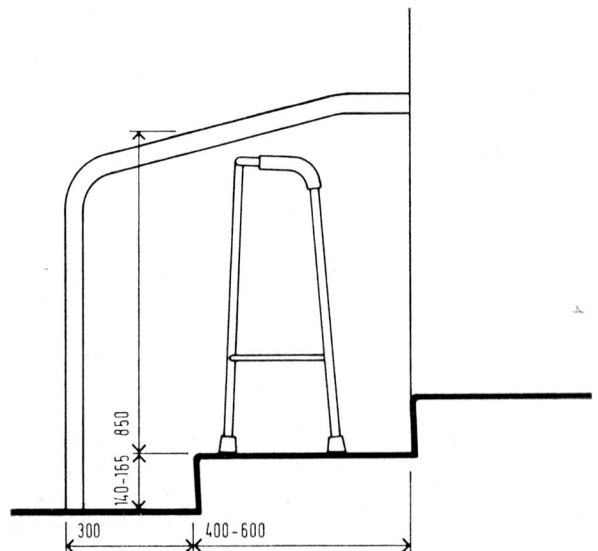

Gently sloping paths and ramps to entrance doors.

Disabled person's dwelling in ground floor flat entered off common stair, close to shops at centre of small town.

Housing for the Disabled

4.4 USE OF FLATTED ACCOMMODATION

4.4.1. Where disabled people are to be housed in flatted accommodation, for instance on the lower floors of a tenement block, communal circulation routes must be designed appropriately for use by them.

4.4.2. Main entrances should be at the same level as any ground floor circulation spaces and lift lobbies, and internal steps should be avoided.

4.4.3. At least one main entrance or exit to each building should be accessible to wheelchair users, and any common door providing an emergency exit or access to a drying area or other external space, and likely to be used by disabled people, should be suitably designed with a level or ramped approach (see 4.3.5.), a flush threshold (see 5.2.3.) and a clear opening width of not less than 775mm. (See 5.2.1.). Double leaf doors should be designed so that only one leaf needs to be opened to meet this requirement. Revolving doors are particularly inconvenient for disabled people and where these are installed a conventional side-hung door of a suitable width should also be provided nearby. At main entrances, automatic sliding doors actuated by pressure pads can be very helpful for disabled people, although this provision would probably be considered extravagant in any but the largest buildings.

4.4.4. Doors in communal circulation areas should have vision panels with the bottom of the glazing no more than 1000mm above floor level for the benefit of wheelchair users. Alternatively, a vertical strip of glass may be inserted on the opening side. Self-closing fire

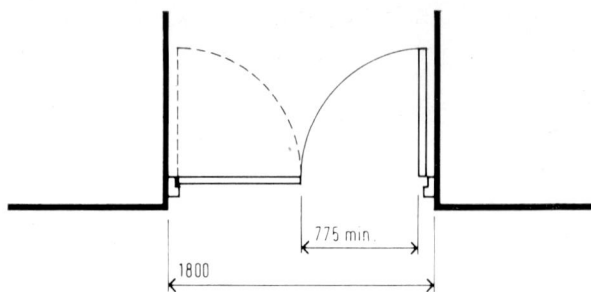

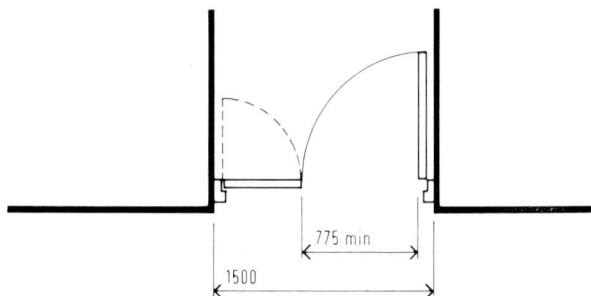

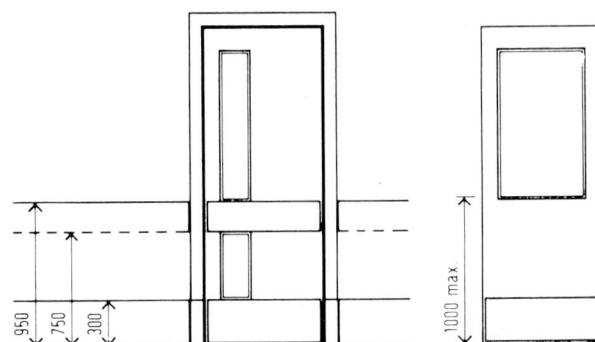

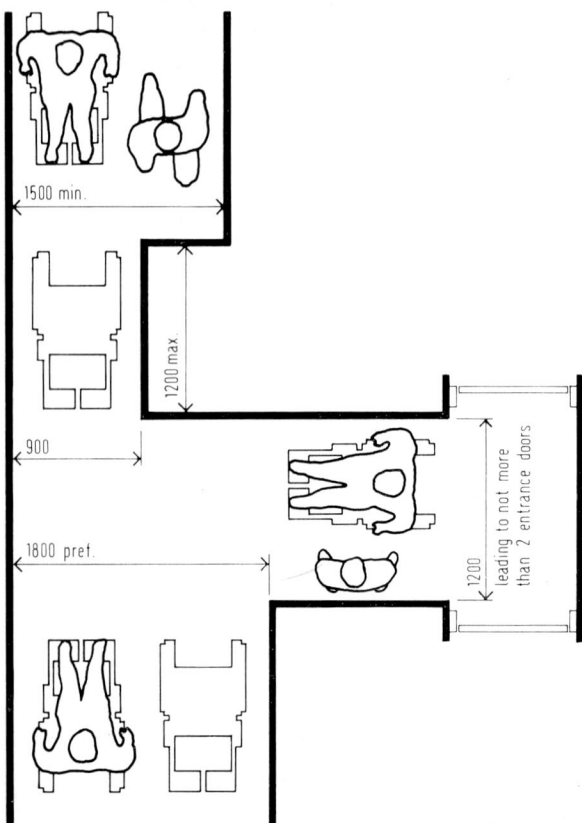

doors in circulation areas should be fitted with stand-open devices which automatically permit the doors to close on actuation of the fire alarm system.

4.4.5. Communal circulation spaces should be at least 1500mm and preferably 1800mm wide to permit two wheelchair users to pass each other. Where a corridor leads to no more than two dwellings the width may be reduced to 1200mm permitting an ambulant person and a wheelchair user to pass. Exceptionally, circulation spaces may be reduced in width to 900mm for distances of no more than 1200mm. Communal circulation areas including lifts (see 3.4.7.) should be equipped with handrails fitted at a height of 950mm. (See 4.3.8.). Damage to wall surfaces by wheelchairs should be prevented by the use of robust finishes with skirtings up to 300mm above floor level in areas of heavy traffic, for instance in common access corridors. Continuous protection in the form of sheet materials up to dado level, or a dado rail 200mm high positioned at 750-950mm above floor level, might also be considered to combat damage which may be inflicted upon wall surfaces by some kinds of wheelchairs which have pushing handles projecting beyond the rear wheels. Corners and arrises should be rounded or protected with the use of specially hardened plaster, profiled strips or angle beads.

4.4.6. Where lifts are provided they should be accessible to wheelchair users and should have unobstructed lobby space at least 1500mm and preferably 1800mm in front of the doors. Wider lobbies may be required where traffic is heaviest at entrance or ground levels. Lifts must not open directly into a corridor or onto a staircase landing but should have a separate lobby between the lift shaft and any other circulation route.

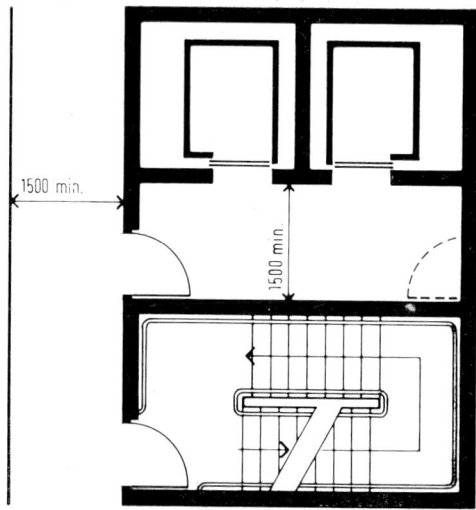

4.4.7. Lift car design should be in accordance with BS2655: Part 3, 1971 'Arrangements of Standard Electric Lifts' with a door giving at least 800mm clear opening width. In buildings used regularly by disabled people, the lift door closing mechanism should have a time delay of at least 5 secs, and the closing speed should not exceed 300mm per sec. A maximum height for lift controls of 1700mm will be satisfactory for most purposes and will generally be accessible for ambulant disabled people. A height of 1350mm is suggested for situations where large numbers of wheelchair users are anticipated. However it should be noted that the lower level is undesirable for general purposes because of the greater danger of misuse by small children.

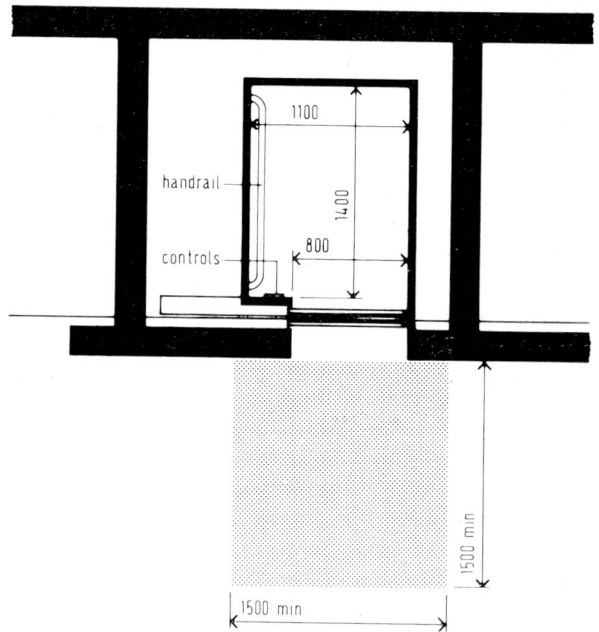

4.4.8. Ambulant disabled people may be housed in multi-storey accommodation provided that adequate lift access is available. It is, however, essential that housing managers are satisfied, after consultation with the appropriate authorities, that the degree of disability of individual tenants in housing above ground floor level will not create dangerous difficulties for the purposes of rescue and exit in emergencies. Because of this and the possibility of breakdown disabled people should not be housed in blocks of flats served by only one lift. It must be remembered that lifts cannot be used as an escape route in the event of fire.

4.4.9. In urban situations disabled people, particularly if they are elderly, may prefer to live on upper levels, rather than on the ground floor where they are likely to be vulnerable to disturbance by vandalism and noise. Ambulant disabled people might therefore suitably be allocated dwellings on upper floors in multi-storey accommodation provided that there is a fire escape stair suitably designed with maximum risers of 175mm and minimum treads of 250mm. Continuous handrails must be provided on both sides of the stair at a height of 850mm from the nosings and extending at least 300mm beyond the top and bottom riser of each flight. Sufficient space should be available on landings or in lobbies at each floor level within the protected zone of the staircase to permit those with limited mobility to safely await the arrival of able-bodied rescuers. People whose mobility is significantly impaired should never be housed in flats above the third floor, which is as far as normal escape ladders

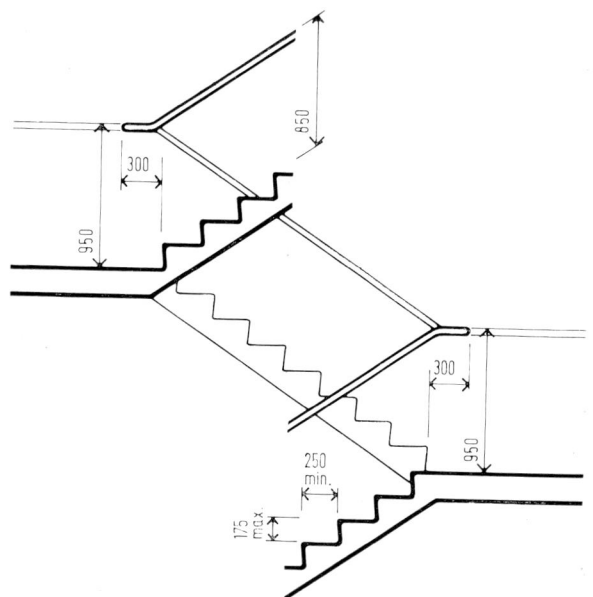

will reach. Handicapped people cannot readily be rescued by the specialised equipment needed for greater heights, and in any case, their physical disabilities may present difficulties for rescuers because of the inability to assist or an impaired sense of balance.

4.4.10. Wheelchair housing should under no circumstances take the form of flats which are without a level or ramped exit to a place of safety. This usually means in practice that they must be located at ground level, although exceptionally it may be possible to provide suitably ramped escape routes from upper floors of buildings on steeply sloping sites where split level access has been provided to a place of safety.

4.5 PARKING AND GARAGING

4.5.1. A car parking space should be provided for each disabled person's dwelling preferably within the curtilage, or in a nearby car parking area with level or ramped access to the dwelling.

4.5.2. Parking spaces should be 4800mm long and 2700mm wide for use by ambulant disabled persons and at least 3000mm wide for wheelchair users. A level or ramped access should be provided from the parking area onto the adjoining pavement or footpath. Car parking spaces reserved for disabled people's vehicles should be clearly indicated with distinctive surface markings or signs.

4.5.3. For wheelchair users the parking space preferably should take the form of a carport or garage and should, if possible, be constructed integrally with or linked to the dwelling, with undercover access provided either by means of doors opening directly from the dwelling or by covered ways or porches. Alternatively, suitably designed garages may be provided in garage courts away from the dwelling provided they are readily accessible.

4.5.4. From the point of view of wheelchair access and manoeuvrability around the car, the carport has certain advantages. The wheelchair user has convenient access to the side doors as well as to the car boot. To achieve equal convenience inside an enclosed

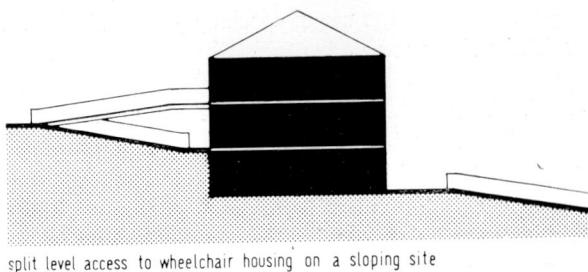

split level access to wheelchair housing on a sloping site

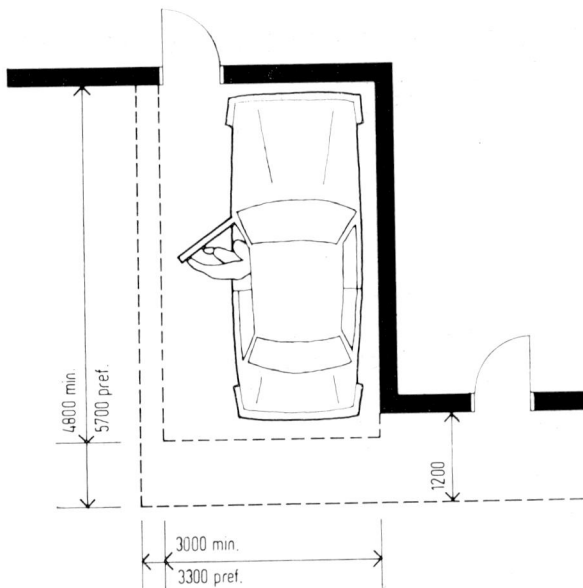

Carport providing covered access to entrance door.

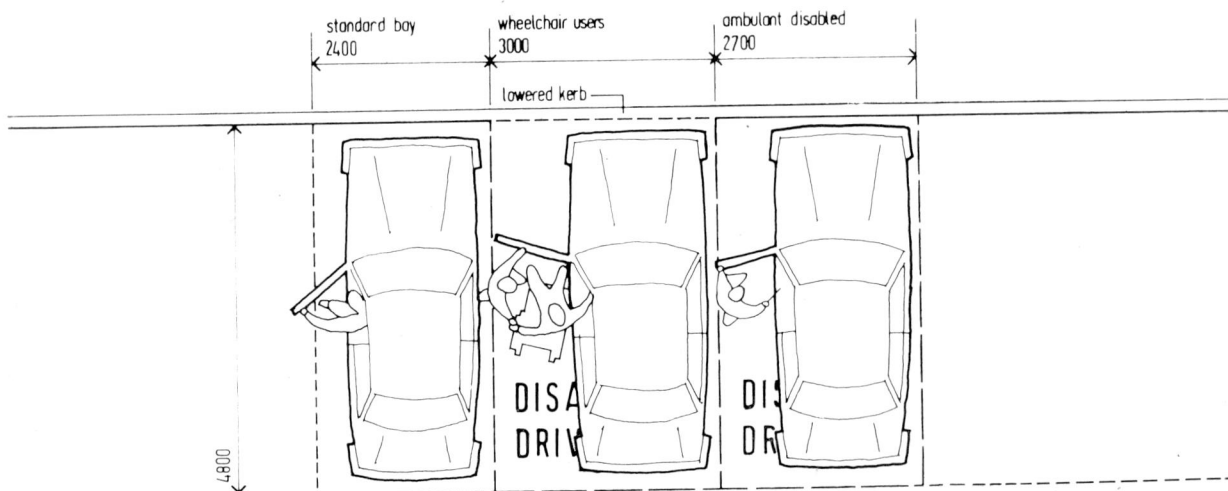

Hardstandings close to dwellings.

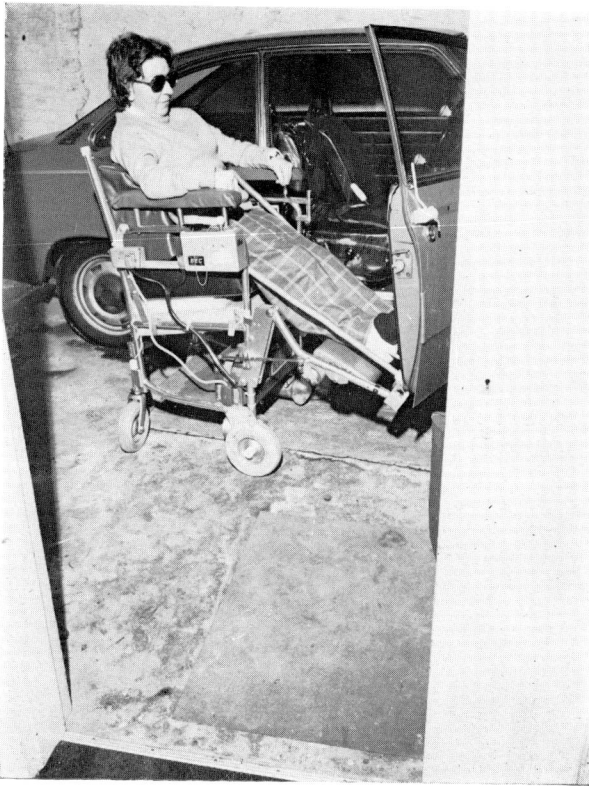

Garage width sufficient to permit wheelchair manoeuvre beside car door.

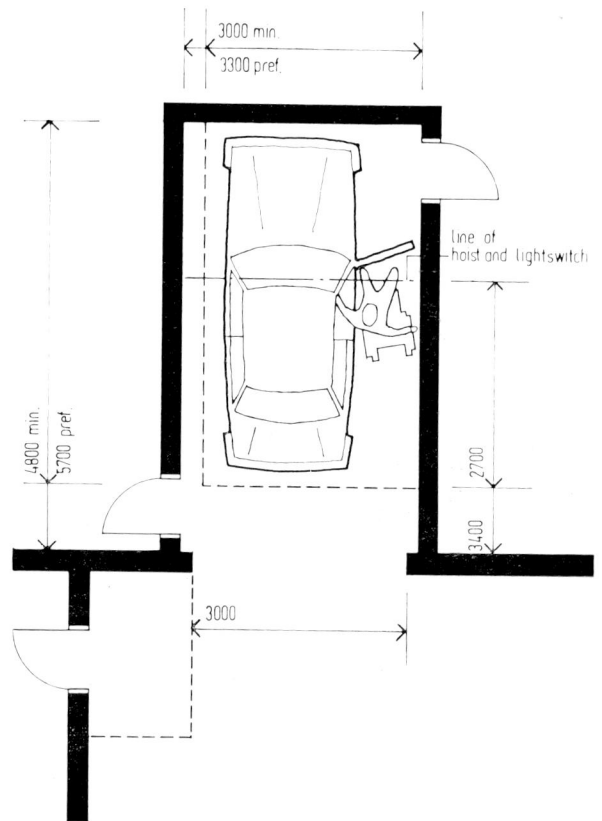

garage would require a very large garage space. The suggested clear undercover area of the carport is 5700 × 3300mm.

4.5.5. Where there is an enclosed garage, the suggested minimum clear space internally is 4800 × 3000mm, and preferably 5700 × 3300mm, allowing entry through the garage door and wheelchair access to the car on one side only. The garage or carport roof should incorporate a cross-beam capable of supporting a stirrup grip or hoist above the car door. A light should be provided operated by a pull-cord located beside the driver's door of the parked vehicle, as well as a switch inside the dwelling or outside the garage door. A power point for a battery charger is required for electrically driven invalid cars and wheelchairs. Garage doors must be easy to operate. Up-and-over doors are preferred but great care needs to be taken in installation to ensure that they are free-running and correctly counterbalanced. Handles for lifting and chain-pulls for lowering must be fitted to the door. A remote control winding mechanism may be helpful for severely disabled people, and electrically driven versions can incorporate a facility for operating the door from within the vehicle.

4.5.6. For wheelchair housing where there is an integral carport or garage, floor levels should be related so as to facilitate access for wheelchair users. Where it is desired to provide a door opening directly between the house and the garage with a flush threshold, the floor of the garage should be laid to a slope of approximately 1:100 away from such a door, in case of oil or petrol spillage. Relaxation from the building regulations, which require a step at the threshold, would need to be sought in order to achieve this amenity, and procedure under schedule 4 of the Building (Scotland) Act 1959 as substituted by the Building (Scotland) Act 1970 should be invoked at an early stage in the design.

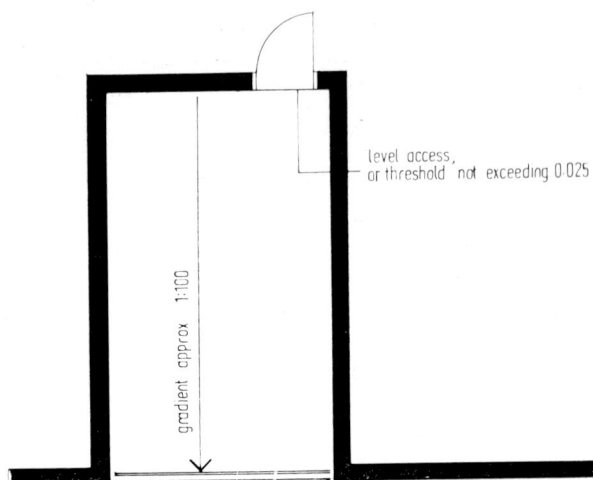

level access,
or threshold not exceeding 0·025

gradient approx 1:100

Garage accessible from inside dwelling, sliding door and flush threshold.

4.6 GARDENS, DRYING FACILITIES AND REFUSE DISPOSAL

4.6.1. Where private gardens are provided in one and two persons dwelling they should be small because handicapped people are unlikely to be able to manage a large plot. Nevertheless, there will always be a proportion of disabled people who enjoy gardening, and there should be some dwellings with suitable facilities within the housing stock. Communal gardens may be provided by the housing authority, particularly in grouped schemes, and maintenance may either become the responsibility of the Parks Department or be organised by a local residents association. Details of such arrangements should be incorporated into house-letting contracts from the outset in order to ensure continuity through subsequent changes in tenancy. Communal upkeep of gardens organised by a housing association or similar private body may achieve excellent results in the quality of landscaping, and some local authority departments have also set exemplary standards of garden maintenance.

Pavement with lowered kerb, ramped up to flush threshold at entrance provides easy and unobtrusive wheelchair access from car.

4.6.2. Garden paths will generally be accessible for disabled people if they are 900mm wide. Turning spaces should also be provided in the layout of gardens for wheelchair housing. A garden path leading from the 'front gate' to the entrance door of the dwelling should be 1200mm wide. Surfaces should be firm and even, and laid to suitably shallow gradients as for public footpaths (see 4.3.5). Where possible a footpath should be provided around the outside of houses to give easy external access between front and back gardens, but hazards, such as ground floor windows which project outwards when open, must be avoided.

4.6.3. For wheelchair users, planting beds on raised terraces or in planting boxes can eliminate many of the problems encountered in garden maintenance. A suitable planting box will be 600-900mm high and not more than 1200mm deep from front to back. There should be a clear space of at least 1200mm in front of the planting box, and it is advantageous if the box can be cantilevered out from a plinth so as to provide a toe recess 300mm high × 175mm deep.

4.6.4. It is especially important for disabled people to have access to any external drying area. Rotary clothes driers may be advantageous in some cases and can be equipped with winding gear to raise or lower the frame thus permitting use by a person seated in a wheelchair. A paved area should be laid around the base of each drier and made accessible by suitable garden footpaths. Adequate drying facilities are essential since there may be extra washing requirements due to incontinence.

4.6.5. Arrangement for refuse disposal must be carefully considered with bins suitably located for easy access by disabled people. In some areas it is normal for bins to be left outside the garden gate on collection days, and this may be extremely difficult or even impossible for disabled people, and local authority Environmental Health Departments should be consulted in order to establish acceptable routines for refuse collection. Communal binstores incorporating palladin containers, may be too high for convenient access by disabled people unless the base of the bins can be set below the floor level of the access lobby, or individual chutes are provided from each flat or landing including the ground floor in multi-storey accommodation. Private binstores are preferred, and these should be located close to the 'back door' of houses. Alternatively, in wheelchair housing bins may be enclosed in a store inside the dwelling accessible from the outside for purposes of refuse collection but having a chute or self-closing hopper from inside the kitchen. Access routes for communal refuse collection must comply with the building regulations which require that footpath gradients on such routes should not exceed 1:14.

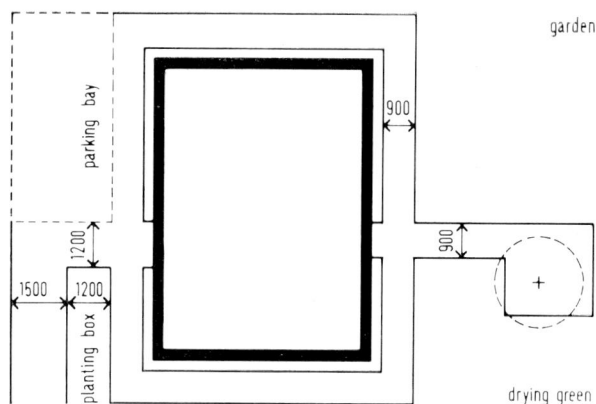

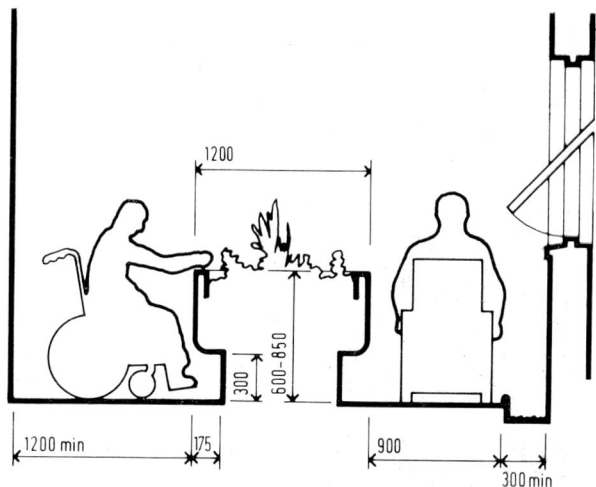

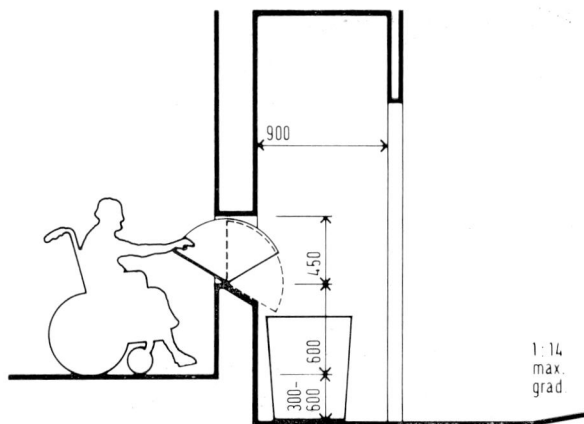

Bin store accessible from inside and outside dwelling.

BIBLIOGRAPHY

4.1 *Integrating the Disabled: Report of the Snowdon Working Party*, The National Fund for Research into Crippling Diseases 1976.

4.1 *Integrated Houses in Haringey: A J Building Study*, Architects' Journal 5 September 1973.

4.1 *Housing for the Disabled in Coventry: A J Building Study*, Architects' Journal 23 October 1974.

4.1 *Housing for the Elderly*, SDD Circular No 120/1975, SED/SWSG Circular No 25/1975.

4.1 *Friendship House, Poole: A J Building Study*, Architects' Journal 29 January 1975.

4.1 *Residential Accommodation for Disabled People: CEH Design Guide* 2, Symons, Centre on Environment for the Handicapped, London 1974.

4.1 *Designing for the Handicapped*, Bayes and Franklin, George Godwin Ltd, London 1971.

4.2 *A Place at work—The Working Environment of the Disabled*, Rogerson and Spence, Scottish Branch of the British Red Cross Society, Glasgow 1969.

4.2 *Providing for the Disabled*, Penton, British Association for Disability and Rehabilitation, English Tourist Board, London 1977.

4.2 *Planning for Disabled People in the Urban Environment*, Planning Research Unit, Edinburgh University, Central Council for the Disabled 1969.

4.2 *Planning for Housing Needs: Pointers towards a Comprehensive Approach*, Scottish Housing Advisory Committee, HMSO 1972.

4.3 *Scottish Housing Handbook, Part 3: Housing Development: Layout, Roads and Services*, SDD, HMSO 1977.

4.3 *The Value of Standards for the External Residential Environment*, DOE Research Report 6, 1975.

4.3 *Access for the Disabled to Buildings, Part 1: General Recommendations*, BSCP 96, British Standards Institute, London 1967.

4.3 *Housing for Disabled People*, EEC Commission Paper V/751/76, EEC, Brussels 1976 (Draft).

4.3 *Design for Access and Mobility*, Australian Standard Code of Practice, Revision of AS CA 52-1, 1968 Standards Association of Australia, Sydney 1975 (Draft).

4.3 *Access for the Disabled: Design Guidance Notes*, Welsh Office, Cardiff 1978.

4.4 *The Building Standards (Scotland) (Consolidation) Regulations*, HMSO 1971.

4.4 *Arrangements of Standard Electric Lifts*, BS 2655: Part 3, British Standards Institute, London 1971.

4.6 *Housing Management in Scotland*, Scottish Housing Advisory Committee, HMSO 1967.

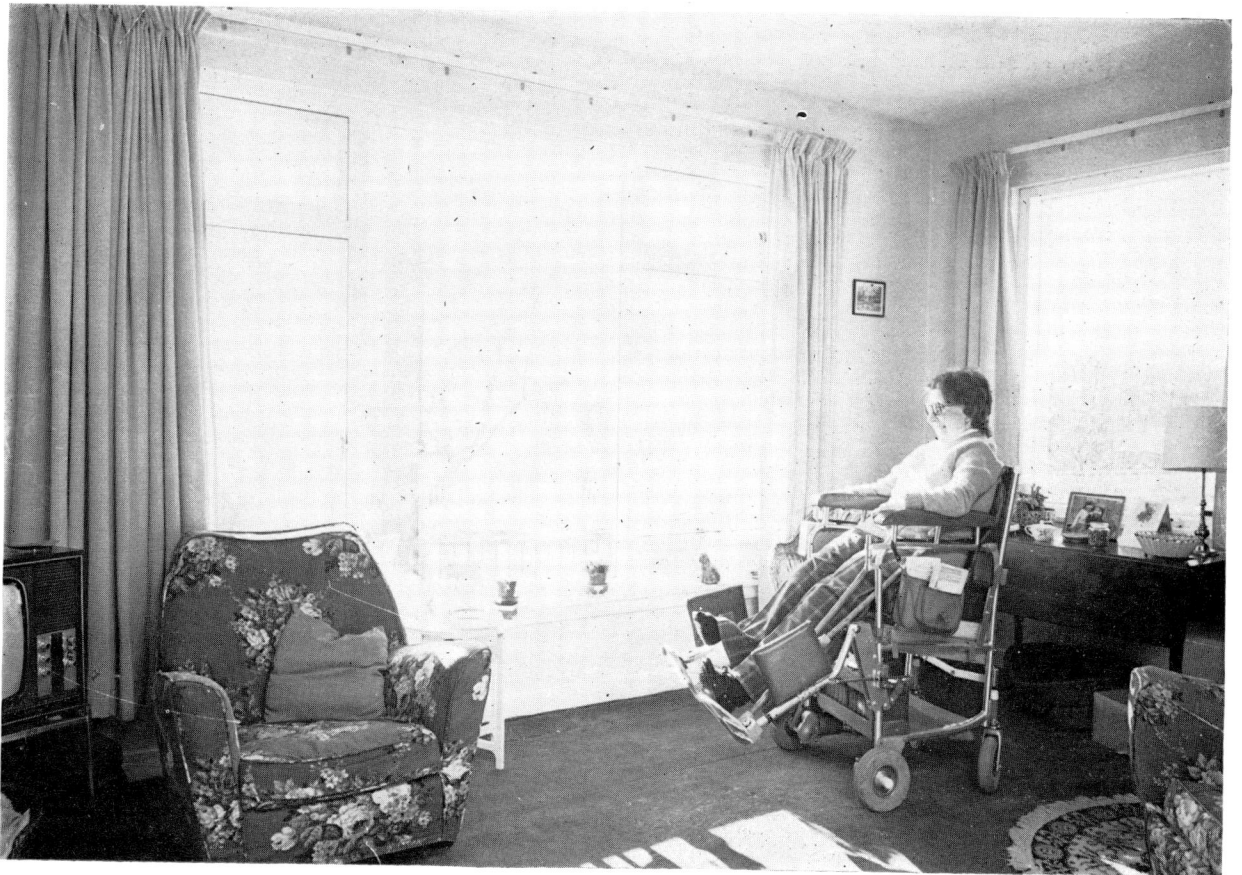

Housing for the Disabled

5.1 SPACE STANDARDS

5.1.1. As indicated previously (1.1.2., 2.2.4.), ambulant disabled people, who form the majority of the population with physical or sensory impairment, can be accommodated satisfactorily in dwellings differing only slightly from ordinary housing and no larger in total floor area. Recommended space standards for ambulant disabled housing are the same as for general needs housing and are set out in the table opposite.

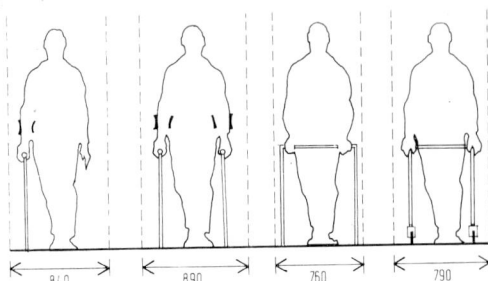

5.1.2. Circulation utilisation spaces for ambulant disabled people using a variety of different types of walking aids are shown in diagrams alongside. From this it will be seen that a passageway width of 900mm commonly used in general needs housing will generally be adequate. In addition, the circulation space provided by use of 900mm wide doorsets in combination with a 900mm wide passage is just sufficient to permit the turning of a wheelchair through the doorways so that occasional use of a wheelchair may be possible in ambulant disabled housing.

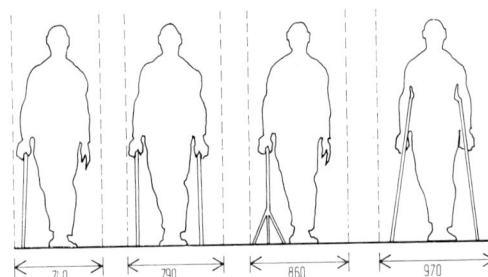

5.1.3. Dwellings for the minority who are severely handicapped must be specially designed to enhanced space standards to take account of the additional floor area necessary for convenient use of wheelchairs particularly in circulation areas and in the bedroom, bathroom and WC. Recommended space standards for wheelchair housing which are approximately 10% higher than general needs housing, are set out in the table opposite.

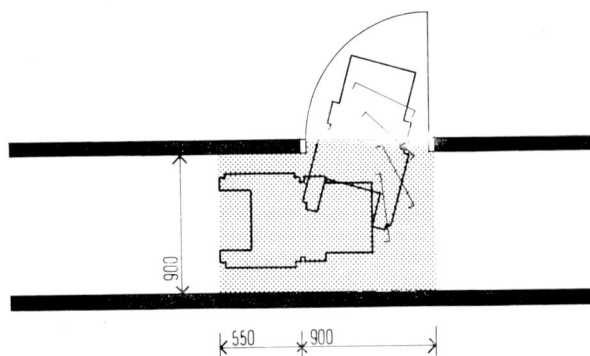

5.1.4. Overall dimensions of a typical NHS standard self-propelling wheelchair in common use, are given in diagrams alongside.

5.1.5. Detailed body measurement data for disabled people is not presented here because of the great caution with which information from the few available sources has to be treated, and the extreme difficulty in obtaining statistically reliable data. Most of the relevant research has been carried out among paraplegics who are not necessarily typical of the severely disabled in that many still retain functional use of their upper limbs. The results of these research projects should therefore be treated with caution when applying them to other types of disability, remembering that a single medical condition does not necessarily create the same degree of handicap in different people.

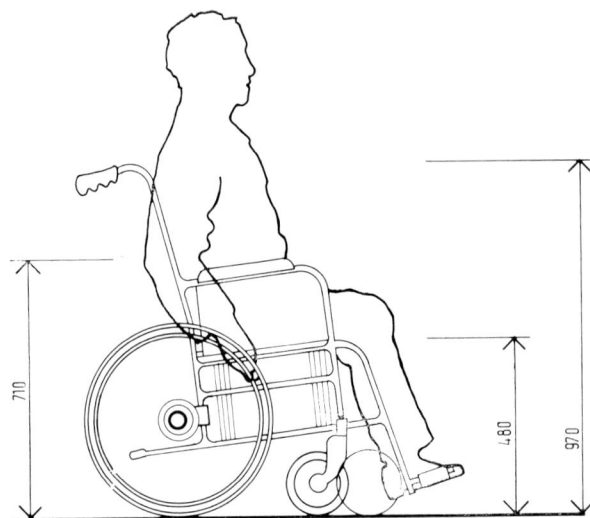

5.1.6. Suggested dimensions or locations of fittings are included in subsequent sections of this part of the Handbook (5.2.-5.10.) to give broad guidance for designers attempting to provide for use by disabled people in general. Where the occupier of a particular dwelling is known, an assessment of the individual's needs should be made by an occupational therapist. Measurement data relating to the disabled occupier should be obtained and, if possible, the occupier should be consulted in person about suitable locations for fittings and heights for shelves or worktops. (See 5.6.3., 5.7.13).

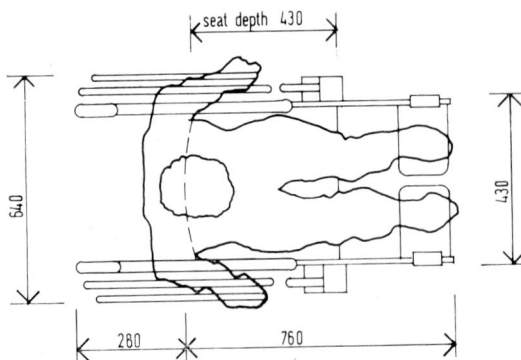

Number of bedspaces per dwelling	Type of Dwelling	Suggested Space Standards Gross Floor Areas m²	
		Ambulant Disabled Housing	Wheelchair Housing
1	Flat	32.5	38.0
	1 storey house	33.0	38.5
2	Flat	47.5	52.5
	1 storey house	48.5	53.5
3	Flat	60.0	66.0
	1 storey house	61.0	67.0
4	Flat	73.5	76.5
	(Balcony Access flat	70.5)	
	1 storey house	71.5	77.5
	(2 storey house	76.5)	
	(2 storey mid terraced house	79.0)	
5	Flat	82.5	89.5
	1 storey house	80.0	90.5
	2 storey house	86.5	95.5
	(2 storey mid terraced house	89.5)	
6	Flat	90.0	98.0
	1 storey house	88.5	99.0
	2 storey house	96.5	106.0
7	2 storey house	114.5	119.5

5.2 ENTRANCE TO THE DWELLING

5.2.1. Openings in external walls for entrance doors to dwellings should be not less than 900mm wide giving a clear opening width of not less than 775mm. (See 5.3.1. and 5.3.2.). This width will be adequate for standard wheelchairs provided that it is not necessary to make a right-angle turn immediately inside the door.

5.2.2. A minimum entrance hall width of 900mm will be adequate for ambulant disabled occupants, and will permit occasional use of a wheelchair. In wheelchair housing the width of the entrance hall should be increased to 1200mm for a distance of at least 1800mm in front of the door, and the door itself should be located to one side so that there is a clear space of at least 300mm beside the leading edge of the front door. This will facilitate opening of the door by walking-aid or wheelchair users. Where a separate entrance lobby is provided with a second door leading into the hall or passageway, or where it is necessary

Flush threshold at entrance door; drainage channel at top of ramp, compressible sealing strip and weather board at lower edge of door.

Housing for the Disabled

for the wheelchair to turn at the entrance door, a space of no less than 1500 × 1500mm is required. Designers should take into account the positioning of heaters or other obstructions which may effectively reduce the space for circulation.

5.2.3. Thresholds at entrance doors should not be higher than 20mm and should preferably be flush. Particularly in exposed situations detailed design solutions to the problem of water penetration should avoid any increase in the height of the threshold. Where a solid ramp is built up to the threshold the vertical damp-proof course should be linked to the weather bar to prevent damp penetration below floor level. A drainage channel covered with a suitable perforated grating may be provided across the outside of the door opening close to the threshold.

5.2.4. Where practicable entrance doors to dwellings should be protected from direct or wind-driven rain by careful choice of dwelling orientation, design of site works for shelter, possible provision of porches, and by setting doors well back from the face of the building.

5.2.5. Where matwells are provided they should be fully recessed. A hard type of mat is preferable because traditional soft coir matting can be a hazard to disabled people using walking aids. A piece of board cut to fit the matwell should be provided so that flooring materials may be laid satisfactorily in the event of the door mat not being used by a particular tenant, but permitting the matwell to be opened up at a later date if required.

5.2.6. In housing for the disabled, the letter box should be located at approximately 750mm above floor level and provided with a mail basket. A deliveries shelf, on which goods may be placed while a disabled occupier is closing the door or manoeuvring the walking aid or wheelchair, should be located at the opening side of the entrance. The shelf should be at least 300 × 300mm and the suggested level is 750mm above floor level. The space underneath must be left clear to facilitate access for a wheelchair user. A similar shelf may also be provided outside the front door in an entrance porch for milk deliveries and newspapers etc. Alternatively, a deliveries box, at approximately 750-1200mm above the floor with two doors or hatches, may be installed beside the entrance. The inner door should always be lockable for security.

5.2.7. Front door locks requiring the use of both hands simultaneously should be avoided and cylinder night latches should be deadlocking to prevent a person being locked out if the door accidentally slams. Mortice deadlocks should be used with caution as they may hinder entry in an emergency by neighbours, or a warden in a sheltered housing scheme, because occupiers frequently leave the key in the locked door thus preventing another key being inserted from outside. Disabled people are frequently conscious of

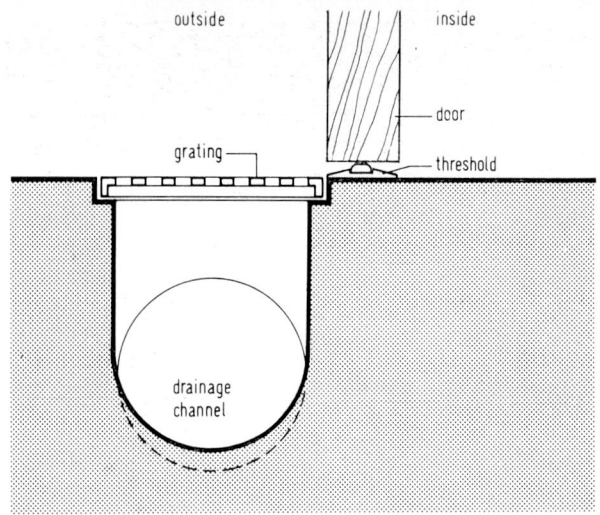

outside   inside

door

grating

threshold

drainage channel

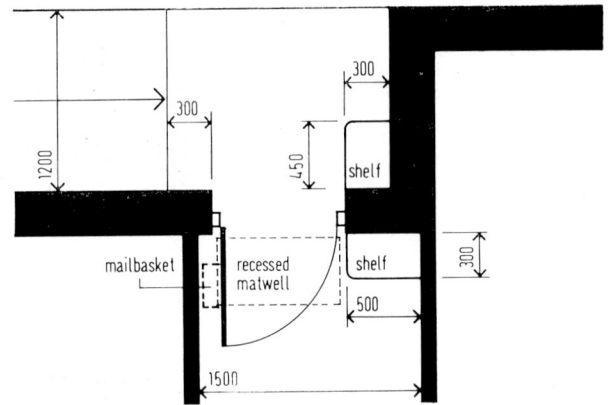

1200   300   300   450   shelf

mailbasket   recessed matwell   shelf   300   500

1500

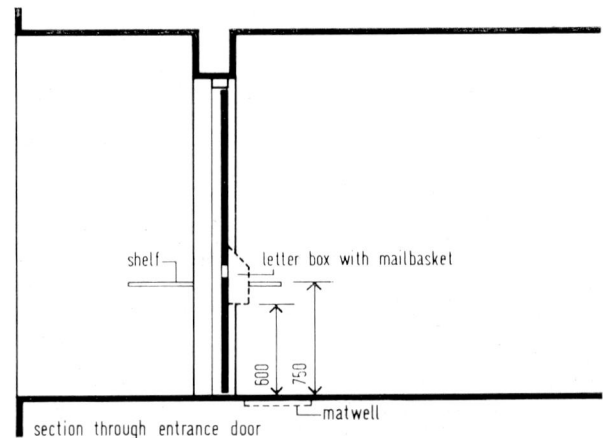

shelf   letter box with mailbasket

600   750

matwell

section through entrance door

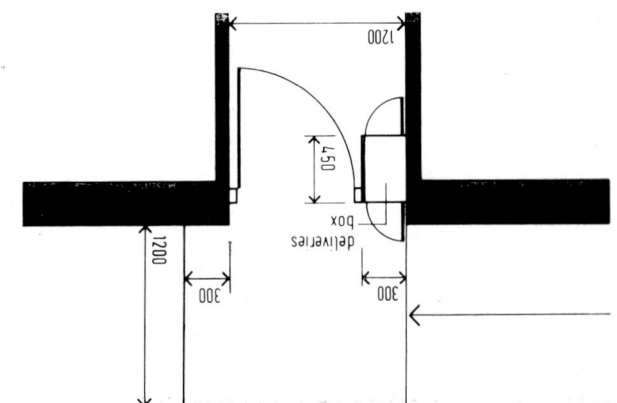

1200   450   deliveries box

1200   300   300

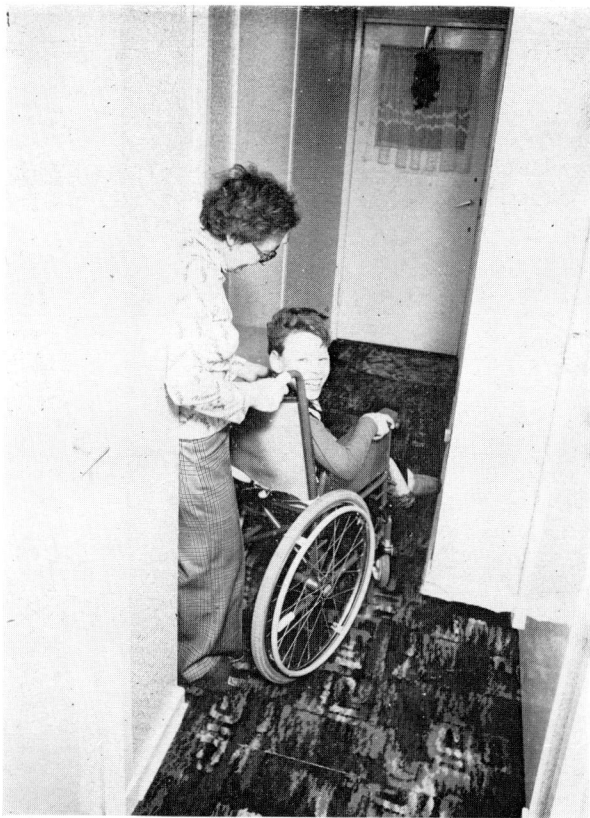

Long narrow halls common in conventional flat plans make wheelchair manoeuvre very difficult.

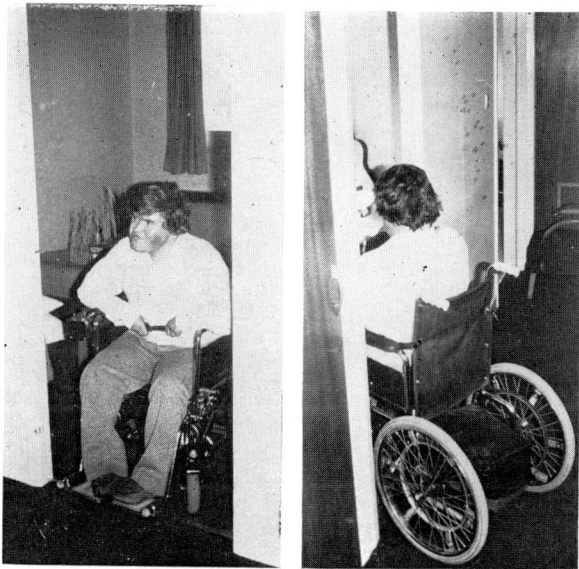

Door to disabled persons bedroom wide enough, but wheelchair user has difficulty in negotiating narrower doors to other bedrooms in the same building.

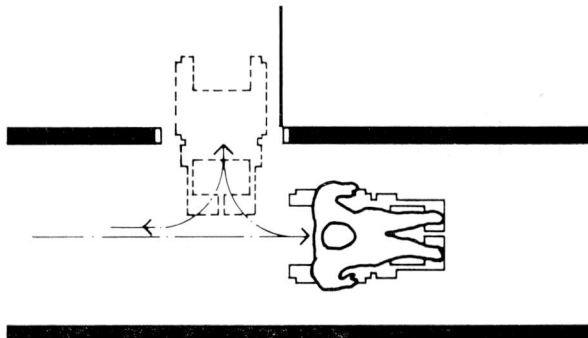

their vulnerability, particularly if they live alone, and a door safety chain might be fitted with advantage.

5.2.8. Mechanical door closers on entrance doors to dwellings from common access and circulation routes can be a severe hindrance to disabled people, particularly wheelchair users. In practice it has been found that one of the first things that a disabled person does on occupation of a flat is to have the door closer removed or disconnected. Where for reasons of increased fire hazard it is essential that the door is self-closing, the mechanism should be supplied with a delayed action stand-open or similar automatic device, having a time delay of at least 5 seconds, to enable an unobstructed passage by disabled persons. However, it is preferable for the closer to be omitted and it may be necessary to apply for a relaxation from the Building Regulations in respect of this item.

5.3 CIRCULATION WITHIN THE HOUSE

5.3.1. Passages inside the dwelling must be at least 900mm wide for ambulant disabled housing. However, for wheelchair housing the required width is 1200mm to facilitate manoeuvring of the wheelchair by a severely disabled person. It will not normally be necessary to provide space for a wheelchair to carry out a full 180° turn as 3-point turns may be executed by making use of doorways. The more generous space standards suggested for wheelchair housing (see 5.1.3.) are largely the result of additional requirements for wheelchair manoeuvre particularly in circulation areas and in bedrooms, bathroom and WC. It is possible that dwelling layouts could make more economical use of space by providing short wide entrance halls rather than long passages. In some housetypes it may even be possible by use of open-planning to incorporate circulation into living areas and to dispense with separate halls or passageways altogether. This approach would permit the individual rooms in the dwelling to be substantially increased in size, within the same overall house shell, and the number of doors to be negotiated would be reduced. However, designers should check unconventional arrangements carefully for compliance with building regulations and in some cases applications for relaxations may be required. (See for example 5.7.14.).

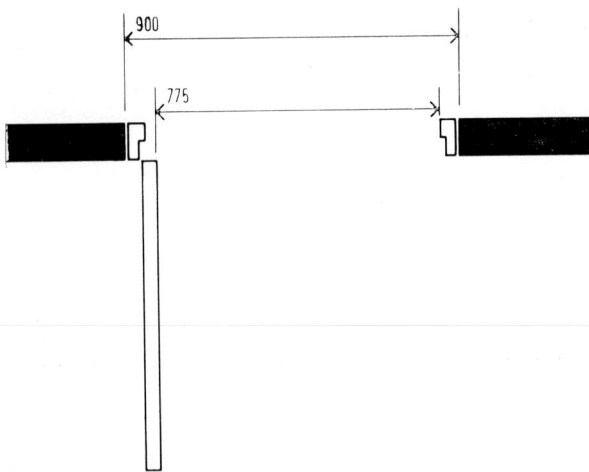

5.3.2. Internal doorsets to all rooms should be 900mm wide, giving a clear opening width of not less than 775mm.

5.3.3. All internal door openings must have flush thresholds. Standard doorsets are normally delivered with threshold pieces incorporated for stability during transit and handling. Specifications should therefore clearly state that these are to be removed to enable floor finishes to be laid flush throughout the dwelling. Some types of equipment such as wheeled walking aids or trolleys have small wheels and door thresholds can severely obstruct movement of these items.

5.3.4. Doors should be located and hung to facilitate manoeuvre of wheelchairs or walking aids with the door handle towards the direction of approach and a clear space of at least 300mm adjacent to the leading edge of the door. This requires the door hinges to be towards the nearest corner of the room which is a reversal of the common practice of hingeing the door away from the corner for reasons of privacy. Doors to small rooms should open outwards into the circulation area but care should be taken to avoid presenting a hazard to people with impaired sight and it is recommended that rising-butt hinges are fitted to such doors. Conflicting door swings should be avoided as far as possible.

5.3.5. In wheelchair housing, sliding doors may be appropriate where it is anticipated that a side-hung door would hinder circulation or wheelchair manoeuvre. However, they are not necessarily preferable and have several disadvantages: sliding doors are generally harder to operate than side-hung doors because of the force required to overcome friction in the mechanism and when in the open position they usually take up valuable wall space at the side of the opening or else require to be housed in a cavity or slot within the thickness of the partition, which may be an expensive detail. The total doorset width required to achieve a given clear opening is generally larger for sliding than for side-hung doors because of the position of the projecting D-handles required for ease of operation. Recessed door handles are considered

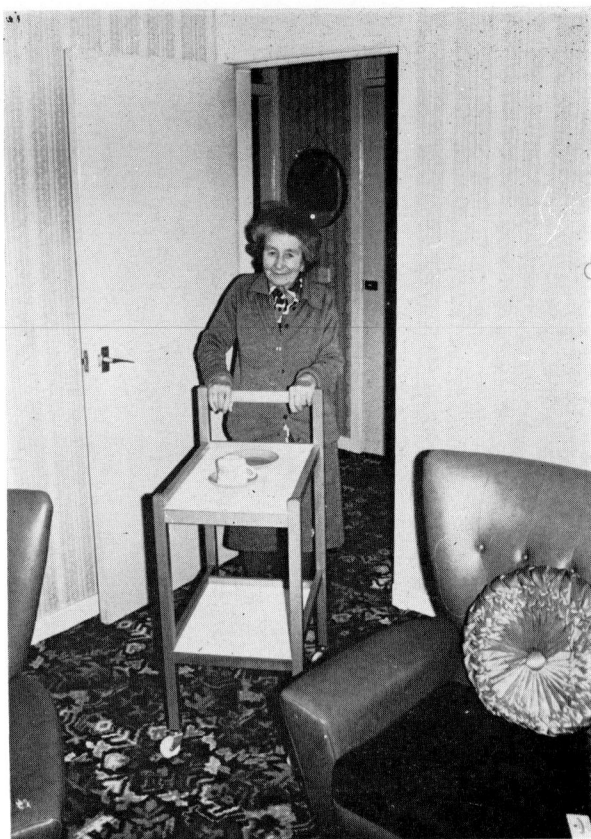

Trolley with raised handle at one end used as walking aid; flush door thresholds.

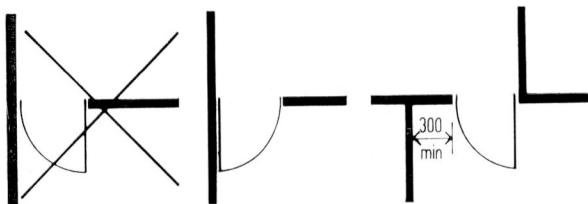

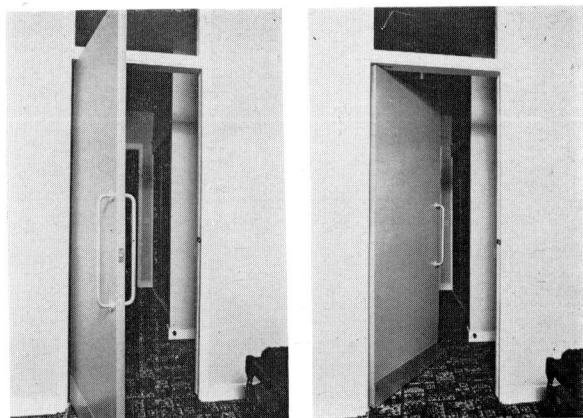

Double swing door between hall and living room; note large pull-handles and position of light switch and socket outlet.

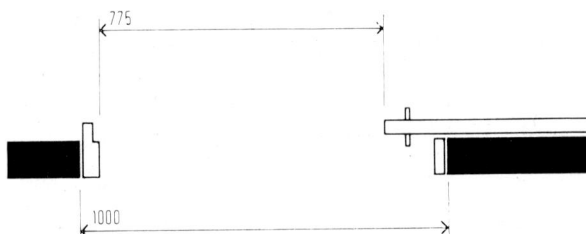

unsuitable for disabled people, especially those with manipulatory problems.

5.3.6. Door ironmongery should be chosen for easy manipulation and sharp edges should be avoided. Lever handles should be used in place of knobs throughout and should be designed so that the end of the handle is turned in towards the face of the door. Door handles should be located between 900-1050mm above floor level. A bold shape, a simple action and a consistent location of door handles can greatly assist the blind or partially sighted. Some disabled people, particularly wheelchair users, may find difficulty reaching to turn a door handle and in such circumstances the normal latch and lever handles can be replaced by a roller catch with push plates and pull handles. For wheelchair users, a useful additional item is a horizontal pull rail, fixed to the trailing side of the door at the same height as the door handle, so that they may close the door as they pass through the opening. Rails or handles used in connection with doors, windows or other equipment should be approximately 25mm in diameter and 35-50mm clear of the surface to which they are fixed.

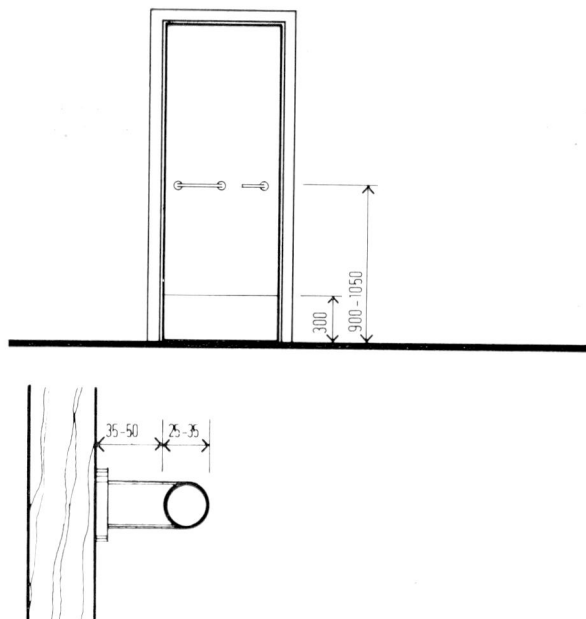

5.3.7. In wheelchair housing it is essential that adequate protection is provided to the trailing faces of doors and jambs with kicking plates or sheet plastic coatings at least 200mm and preferably 300mm high. Protection should also be provided to external corners

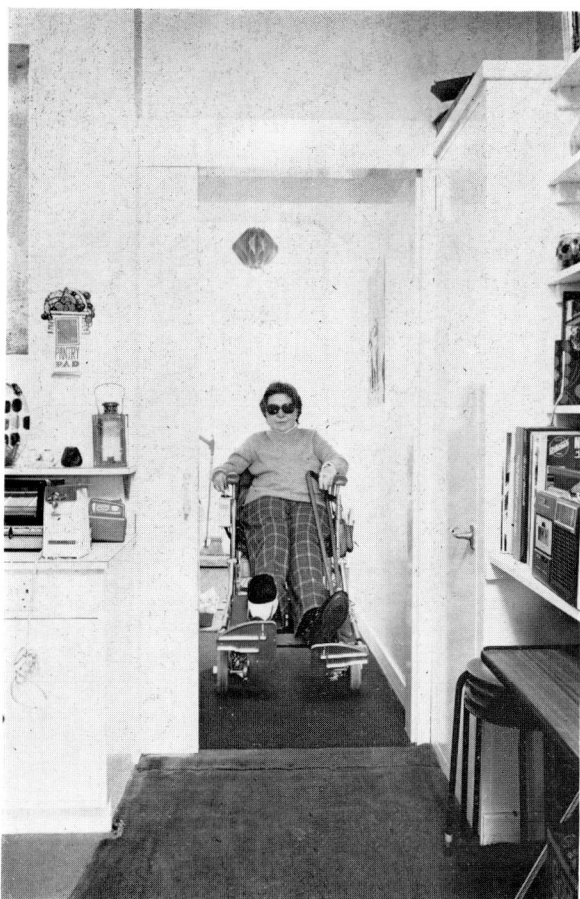

A sliding door may be useful in some circumstances, especially where circulation space is limited.

of partitions, for example with profiled strips or with angle plaster beads and a hard plaster specification.

5.3.8. It is anticipated that disabled people's housing will normally be designed on one level since it is obviously advantageous if the disabled member of the household can gain access to every room. However, larger dwellings on two storeys may be suitable provided that the bathroom and bedroom used by severely disabled persons are at entrance level. Exceptionally, two storey dwellings may be suitable for occupation by ambulant disabled people provided that there is at least a WC at entrance level and a straightflight staircase with clear landing at top and bottom permitting the installation of a mechanical stairlift at a later date, if necessary. Stairlifts may take the form of either a simple seat attached to the lifting mechanism at one side of the stair or a large platform onto which the occupant's wheelchair can be manoeuvred. Alternatively, a separate vertical hoist may be installed. These types of appliances tend to be rather expensive and would not generally fall within the scope of housing provision although social work departments may be able to have them installed in some special circumstances. Care should be taken in the selection of any such equipment to ensure that it incorporates fail-safe devices which will arrest the motion of the lift in case of accidental or incorrect operation of the lift. Stairs should have maximum risers of 175mm and minimum treads of 250mm. Handrails should be continuous and allowance made for the fixing of an additional handrail on the other side of the stair if required.

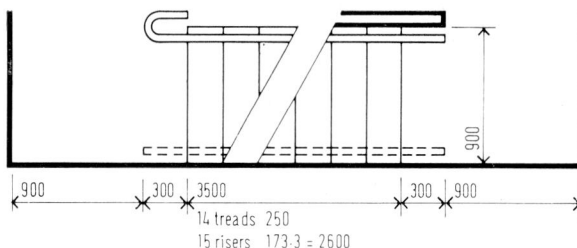

5.4 LIVING ROOM

5.4.1. Designers of housing for disabled people should always bear in mind the large proportion of time spent in the living room by severely handicapped people, particularly if they are also elderly, and the importance of providing a comfortable, pleasant and convenient environment for them.

5.4.2. It is expected that many of the younger disabled people will go out to work or to a day care facility, but others may have occupations which can be carried out at home. In the latter event either part of the living room would be used for work, which would require additional space, or one of the bedrooms might be used as a work room. Additional space may also be required in living areas for temporary storage of large items of equipment.

5.4.3. In wheelchair housing, furniture layout should be arranged with circulation and manoeuvring of a wheelchair in mind. There should always be an unobstructed route from the door to the centre of the room where sufficient clear space is provided to turn the wheelchair through 180°. In practice, the wheelchair user will be able to carry out 3-point turns in relatively confined spaces using gaps between furniture or door openings. However, as a general guide, a 1500mm diameter circle superimposed on a furniture layout plan will give a crude but effective indication of the space required for turning, even though the wall-to-wall 360° turning circle for some types of wheelchairs may in fact be larger than this. (For more detailed information see paragraph 5.1.4).

5.4.4. The orientation of the dwelling and the design of the living room window should permit a seated person to enjoy interesting views of the outside world. Sills should be approximately 600mm above floor level and transom heights should avoid the range 1000-1350mm, so as not to interrupt the line of sight at eye level for a seated person. Furniture should not be positioned in front of main windows, so that the disabled occupier may approach close to the windows for purposes of viewing, opening or cleaning. A bay window providing alternative views from the living room of a disabled person's dwelling would be a most desirable feature. They should provide good ventilation at high and low levels, and controls should be placed within reach of a seated person for ease of operation. The window should also be selected for ease of cleaning as well as its quality of performance in use. Care should be taken with the choice and location of outward opening ground floor windows to avoid creating a safety hazard for people moving past outside (see 4.6.2.). It is advantageous for purposes of window cleaning if access can be provided all round the outside of the dwelling. However, public footpaths should not be located immediately adjacent to the windows for reasons of privacy. If it is proposed to incorporate lowered sills to living room windows in flats, the design of the windows should take into account the

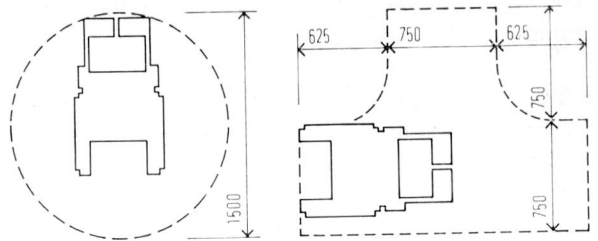

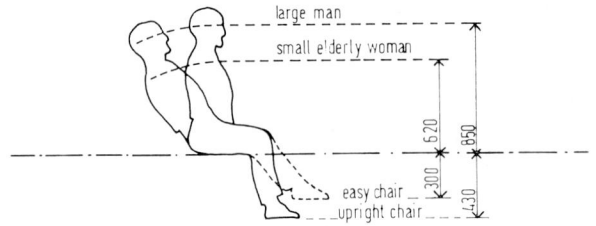

Living room window-sill too high for seated person to see out.

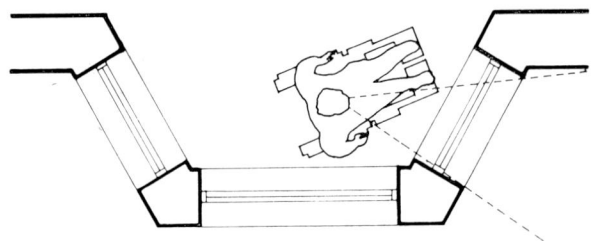

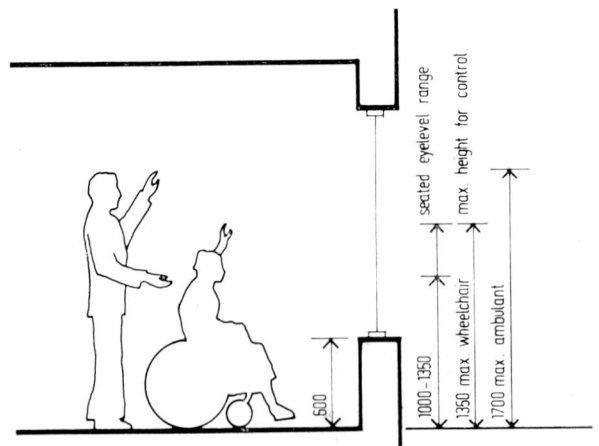

need to avoid excessive flanking sound transmission vertically between dwellings.

5.4.5. Ironmongery should be robust with large operating handles for ease of manipulation. For the severely disabled person with limited reach it is desirable that some form of remote control gear can be used. This may take the form of a lever or winding mechanism connected to the window with rods or flexible cable. This is particularly useful if there are high level opening lights, or ventilators are incorporated in slots at the top of the windows. Windows may also be cord operated.

5.5 BEDROOM

5.5.1. In ambulant disabled housing it is only necessary that bedrooms should be *accessible* for occasional wheelchair users and there is no need for an increase in floor area. In such a case the wheelchair will be able to enter forwards and reverse out provided that the general requirements for circulation are satisfied. (See 5.3.4).

5.5.2. Specially designed wheelchair housing, on the other hand, should have at least one bedroom at entrance level designed to be independently *usable* by severely handicapped people in wheelchairs, not merely accessible. The layout should provide an unobstructed turning area of 1500mm diameter within the room and a clear space of 1200mm in front of any storage cupboards, wardrobes, or chests of drawers.

5.5.3. The design of clothes storage facilities should be considered with the needs of the disabled in mind. (See 5.8.4). In wheelchair housing, built-in wardrobes

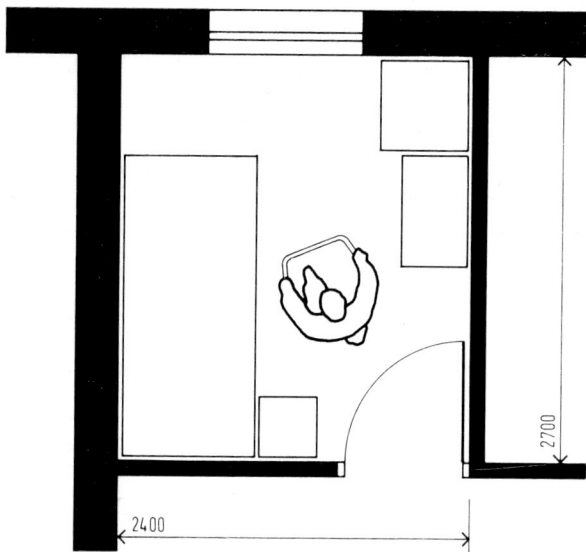

typical single bedroom layout suitable for the ambulant disabled

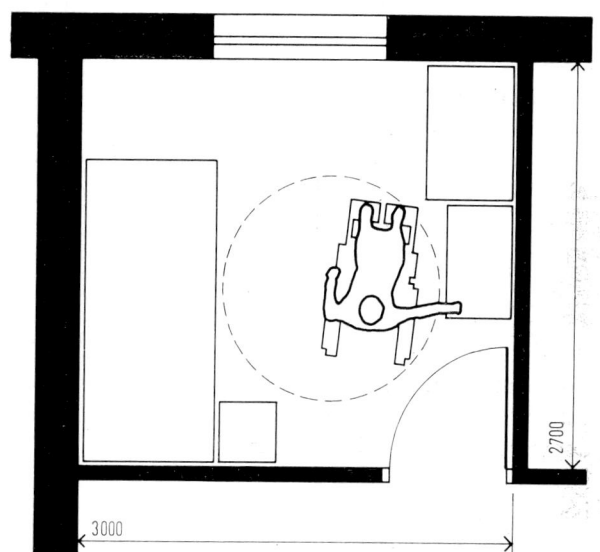

similar bedroom enlarged to provide space for full wheelchair use

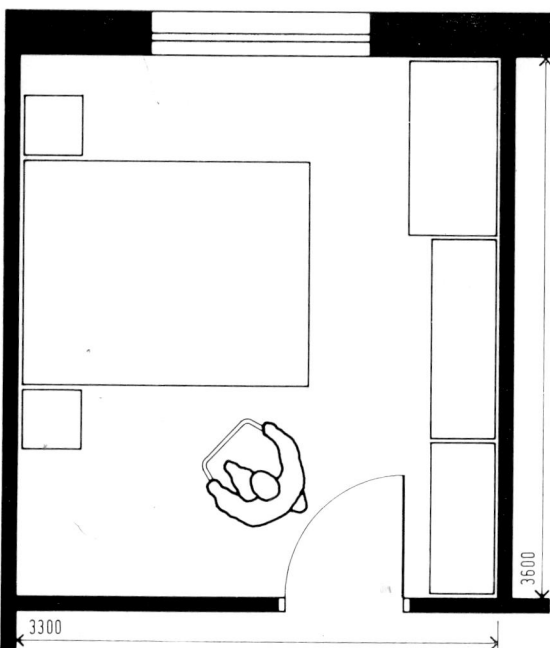

typical double bedroom layout suitable for the ambulant disabled

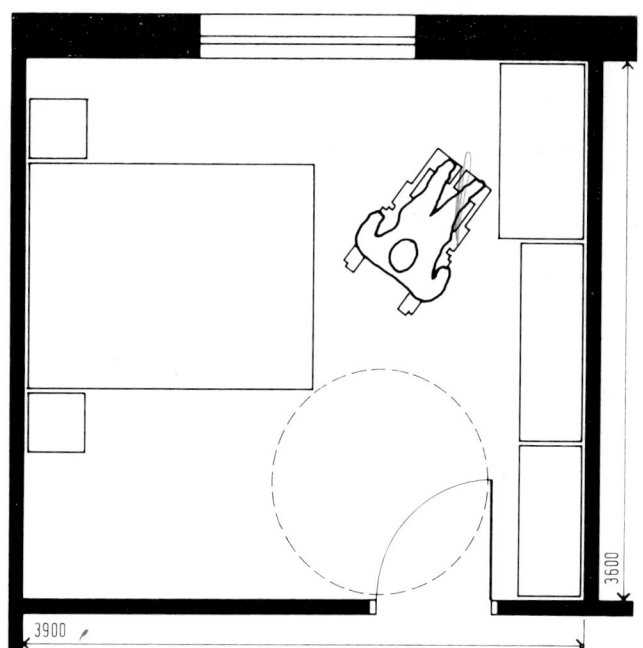

similar bedroom enlarged to provide space for full wheelchair use

Housing for the Disabled

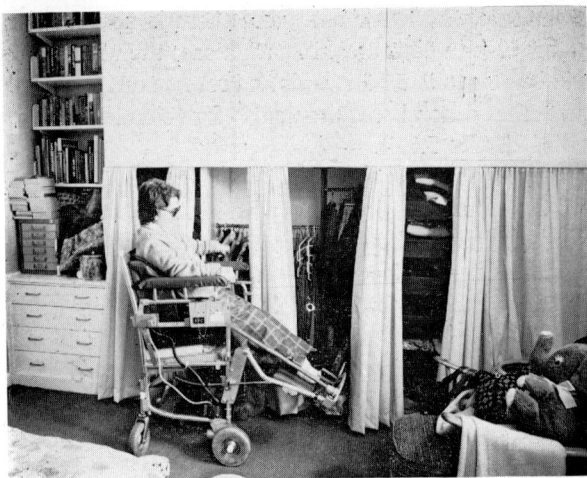

Curtains facilitating access to wardrobe space.

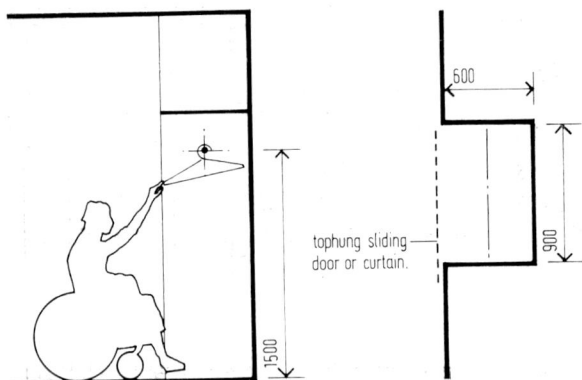

should have top-hung sliding doors in preference to side-hinged doors which tend to obstruct access from a wheelchair or walking frame. Bottom rolling sliding doors should be avoided because the rail may cause an obstruction. Clothes hanging rails should preferably be located at about 1500mm above floor level and should be fixed in such a way that the height is readily adjustable to suit the individual occupier.

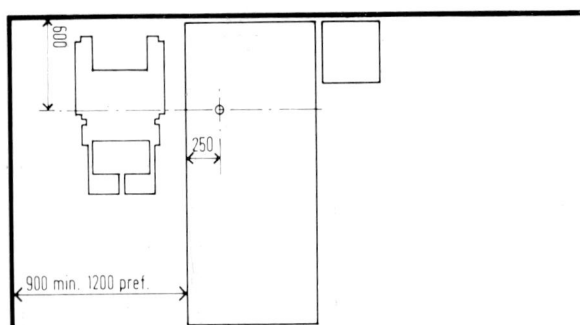

5.5.4. Ceiling construction in wheelchair housing should be such as to permit the installation of stirrup grips or hoists, if required. It should be remembered that tenants rarely place furniture in the precise location indicated on designers' layout plans and it is advisable to leave fixing of such items until the requirements of a particular occupier are known. (See 5.7.14).

5.5.5. High bedroom window sills are often specified for reasons of privacy, but, where a disabled tenant might be bed-fast, it is desirable to provide a lower sill so as to afford a view of the outside world for the

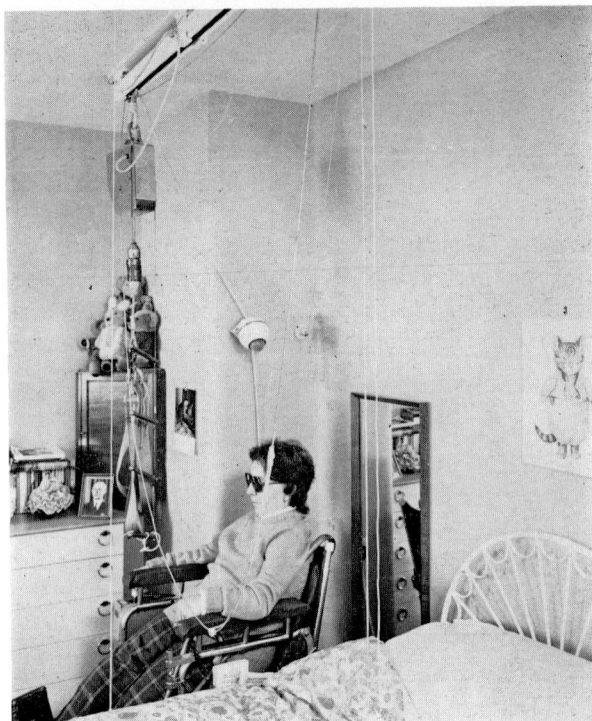

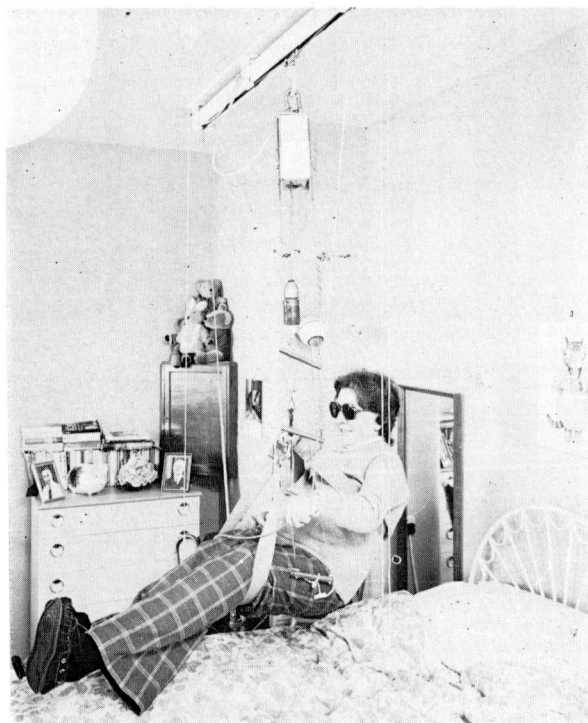

Space required in bedroom for transfer from chair to bed using ceiling mounted hoist.

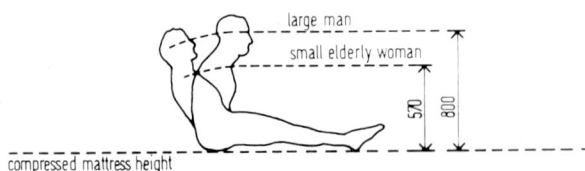

occupant of the room seated in bed. A height of 900mm above floor level is suggested. It should be remembered that privacy may be readily obtained by use of net curtains, whereas it would be much harder to increase the size of the window.

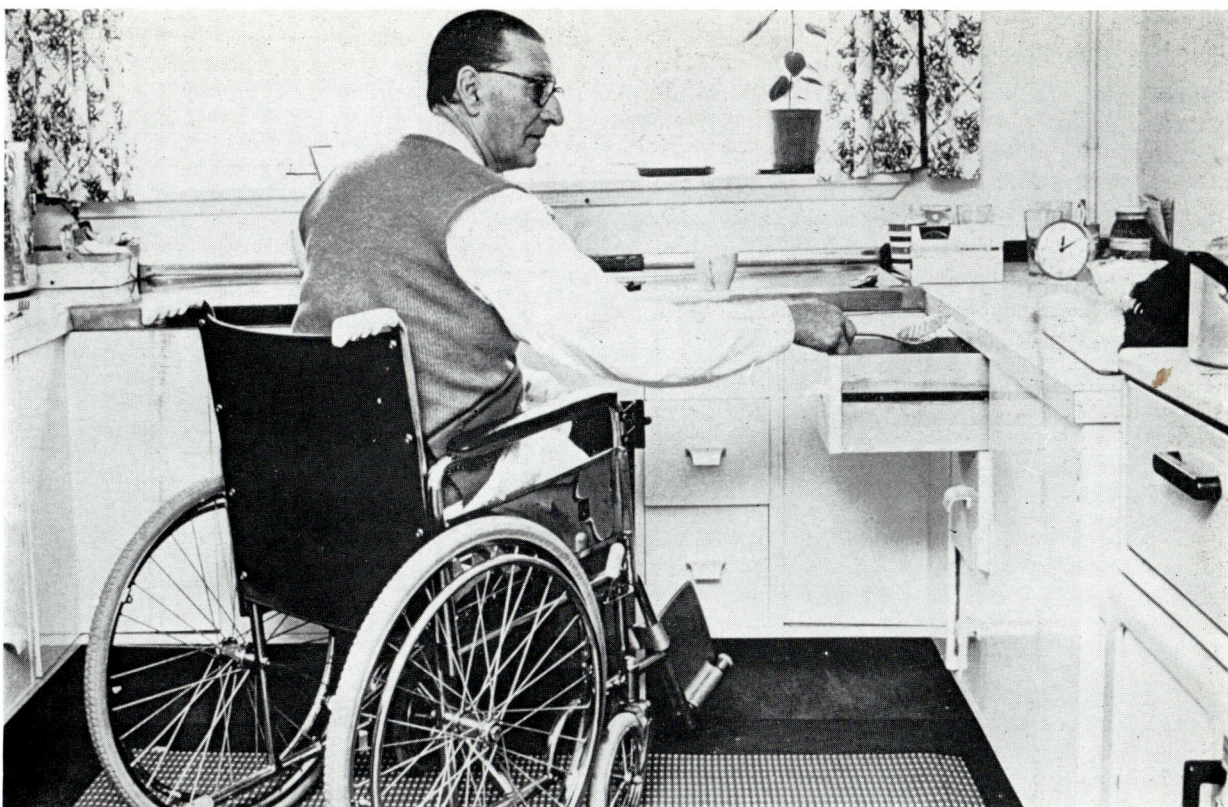

U-shaped kitchen permits wheelchair user to reach all equipment with minimum movement.

5.6 KITCHEN

5.6.1. In the planning and design of kitchens for use by disabled people particular attention must be paid to providing a convenient layout of fixed furniture, fittings and equipment. It is generally preferable for specific activities to occur in spaces not traversed by circulation routes. The usual unbroken sequence of units comprising worktop/sink/worktop/cooker/worktop is recommended and the layout may either be L-shaped or U-shaped provided that there is a clear wheelchair turning space of at least 1500mm between opposite worktops or between a worktop and a wall. Long narrow kitchens with a clear space of only 1200mm may also be suitable provided that there is an open space beneath the worktop to permit a wheelchair to perform a 3-point turn.

5.6.2. In new housing, dining areas are commonly combined with kitchens and this is certainly convenient for serving and clearing up after meals although not so satisfactory for entertaining visitors, when a living/dining room or a separate dining room is generally preferred. Combined kitchen/dining or living/dining rooms can be advantageous for households with a disabled member as space is more readily available for manoeuvring a wheelchair or walking-aid for approach to the table. Where a separate dining room is provided or there is a living/dining room, space should still be provided in the kitchen for at least two people to take a casual meal.

5.6.3. Standard worktops are normally 600mm deep, although some shallow types 500-525mm deep

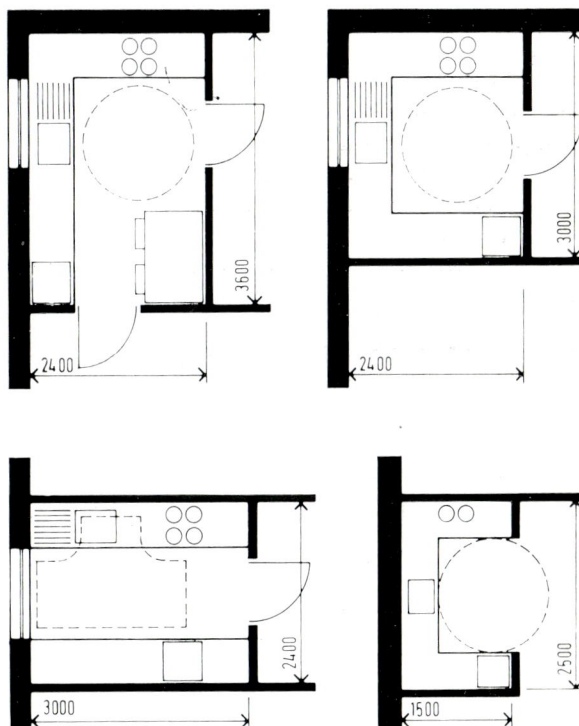

are available for use where an occupier has difficulty reaching across. The space at the back of a deep worktop, out of easy reach for working, will frequently be used for storage of equipment and this may be convenient where a disabled person is unable to make full use of high level cupboards. The worktop should overhang the front of any base units to provide an edge or lip for gripping and support. Standard worktop height is 900mm which will be suitable for the majority of ambulant disabled people. In wheelchair housing,

Housing for the Disabled

a height of 800-850mm will be more appropriate for very short or frail people, or severely disabled people. The choice of height will depend very much upon the requirements and capabilities of the individual occupier and, particularly in family dwellings, the extent to which the disabled person actually works in the kitchen. Generally it is assumed that at least hot drinks and snacks will be prepared by a disabled person even if main meals are prepared by another member of the family or a home help, for whom a lowered worktop would be very inconvenient, or are delivered by community services.

5.6.4. It is therefore essential that in wheelchair housing the design of the kitchen furniture should permit some flexibility in worktop height to suit different circumstances. One solution is to have the worktops, and storage units where these are linked, mounted on adjustable brackets and slotted wall channels. A number of different heights would then be possible and a variety of levels could be provided where kitchens are used by able-bodied as well as disabled people. Instant adjustability in the height of equipment or work surfaces, to cater for use by different people during the course of each day, would be very difficult to achieve economically. If this degree of flexibility is essential, a more practical solution to the problem might be for the severely disabled person's wheelchair to be fitted with a raise/lower device.

5.6.5. If, for reasons of economy, the worktop has to be fixed in advance and cannot be made adjustable, sections of worktop at different heights may be provided to permit use of kitchen equipment by persons either seated or standing. Some manufacturers can supply alternative plinths for base units in order to achieve height adjustments, and this could be a

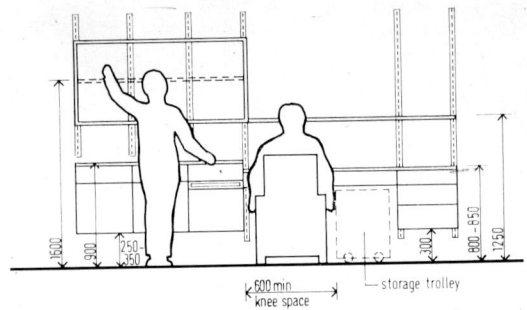

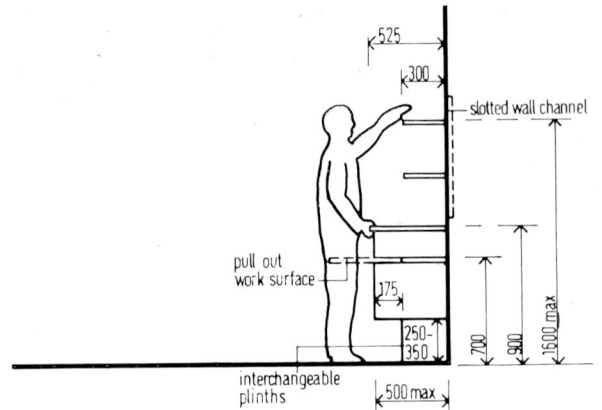

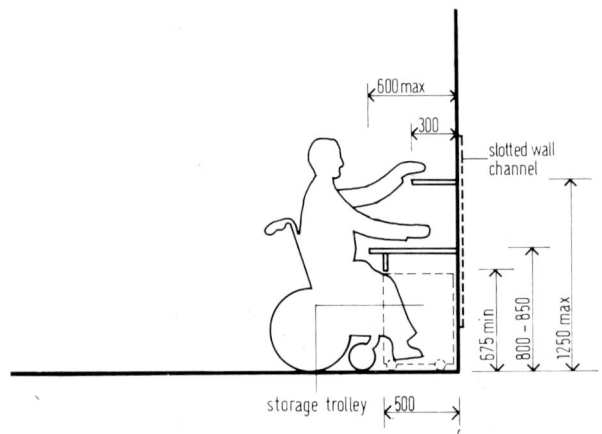

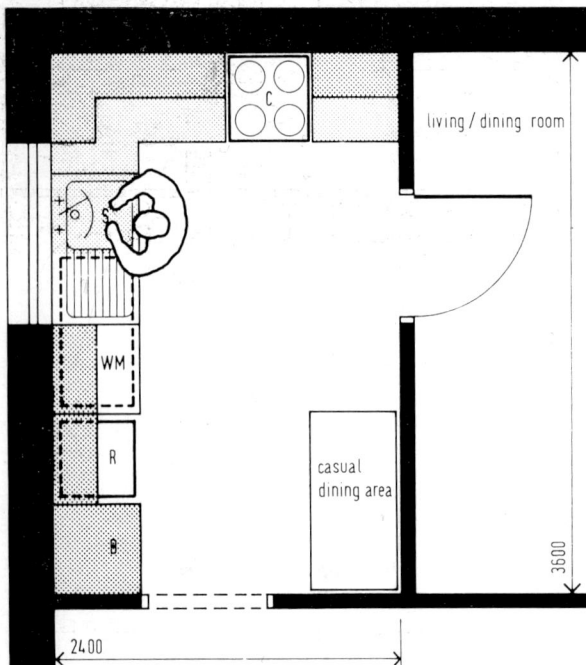

typical standard kitchen layout appropriate for ambulant disabled housing
light tone signifies storage below worktop level
dark tone — high level storage units

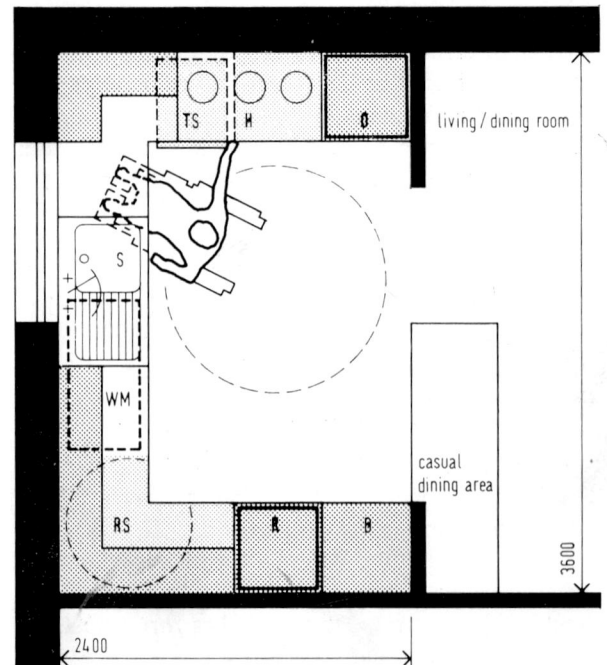

similar kitchen layout amended to suit a wheelchair user
O — oven   H — hob   C — cooker   TS — trolley storage unit   B — broom cupboard
WM — washing machine   R — refrigerator   RS — rotating storage unit   S — sink

satisfactory solution in ambulant disabled housing. (See 5.8.1).

5.6.6. The incorporation of storage units can pose problems as the ability of disabled people to reach up or stoop may be limited. (See 5.8.2). In wheelchair housing, location of low-level storage units must be considered carefully so as to provide adequate knee-space at the key working stations. Knee-spaces should be not less than 750mm wide × 675mm high × 500mm deep. High level units should be not more than 300mm deep and low level units no more than 500mm deep. Storage cupboards should be flexible in positioning for height, with adjustable fixing brackets and slotted wall track or alternative plinth heights. Flexibility in layout may be provided by having some base units on castors. These may then be pulled out from under the worktops for ease of access and to provide a working surface at a lower level. Revolving cupboards in corner positions and storage racks hung on the inner face of side-hung cupboard doors can be helpful. Fixed base units should be provided with large toe-recesses at least 300mm high × 180mm deep. Pull-out work surfaces at a height of about 700mm, giving a clear height underneath of not less than 675mm, should be provided below worktops in storage units at either side of the main preparation area. These should be suitable for chopping or may incorporate circular apertures to hold bowls during mixing or beating operations. Pull-out boards must be designed in such a way as to prevent them from being withdrawn accidentally while in use, although the fixing should permit them to be removed when necessary for cleaning purposes.

5.6.7. Refrigerators should be raised off the floor on plinths or mounted in a range of kitchen storage units in such a way that the bottom shelf is at least 300mm above floor level for wheelchair users and 500mm for ambulant disabled persons. The top of the refrigerator should be no higher than 1350mm for wheelchair users or 1700mm for ambulant disabled. The location of the refrigerator and the handing of the door should be chosen with regard to ease of circulation within the working area of the kitchen.

5.6.8. The cooker should preferably have a separate hob and oven supported in such a way that the most convenient level may be chosen for each item of equipment. This type of split level arrangement is ideal for wheelchair dwellings as a knee-space may thereby be provided underneath the hob. The arrangement can also be suitable for ambulant disabled

Kitchen storage provided in full height units; note door handles at high and low levels and large toe recesses.

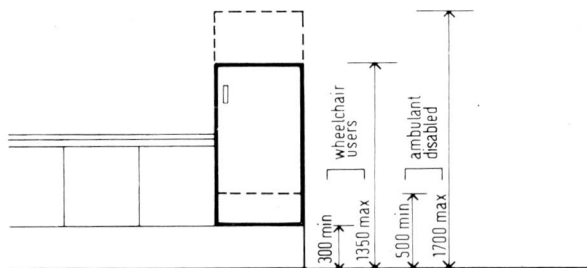

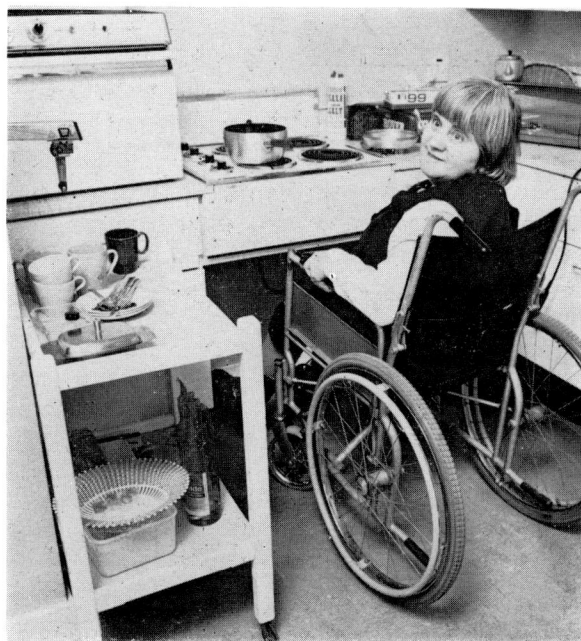

Separate oven at worktop level and hob with knee recess below permits access by wheelchair user.

people who may have difficulty stooping to reach the oven in a conventional cooker. However, the shelf or section of the worktop supporting the hob should be designed so that it can easily be removed if the

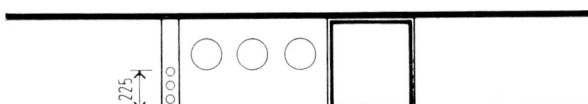

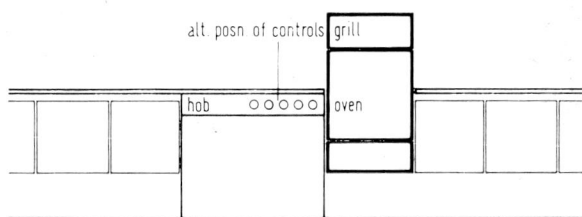

occupier prefers a conventional cooker. The hob should be located so that the surface of the hot-plates are at exactly the same level as the worktop on either side. If the hob is built in to the worktop it is advantageous if some of the rings can be set back 225mm from the front edge of the worktop for minor preparation and safe transfer of pans. The oven should be located so that the middle is aligned with the worktop. The grill may be incorporated with either the oven or the hob. For ease and safety of access for the disabled person, controls should never be positioned above or behind the hob, but they should be located out of reach of children particularly in family dwellings.

5.6.9. Ideally, the sink and drainer should be adjustable for height and this may be achieved by setting the unit into a worktop supported on adjustable fixing brackets and vertical slotted channels in the same way as the storage cupboards. It may be possible for pipework connections to be made with sections of flexible hose, but designers should discuss this item with local Building Control Departments and Water Authorities before installation. Alternatively, if rigid pipes were essential, various different lengths of connectors could be provided so that final fixing of the sink could be left until the tenant was known. Rim height of the sink will generally be between 800mm and 900mm above floor level. Deep sinks are undesirable particularly for wheelchair users and the recommended depth is 150-175mm. Square or rectangular sinks are preferable to circular or elliptical shapes for the purpose of dishwashing. In wheelchair dwellings a clear knee recess preferably 900mm wide × 500mm deep × 675mm high should be provided under the sink and drainer. Care should be taken in the plumbing layout to avoid excessive intrusion of pipework into the knee recess. It is essential that the under side of the sink bowl and any exposed pipes be coated with insulating material to avoid burns for those with reduced sensory functions.

5.6.10. Taps should be selected for ease of manipulation, and metal capstan or lever taps are preferred to cylindrical types. In some cases remote control taps operated below the front edge of the worktop may be suitable. Swivel spout mixer taps are also desirable and should be offset for ease of filling pans and kettles.

5.6.11. Care should be taken to avoid slippery floor finishes in the kitchen.

5.6.12. It is particularly important where there may

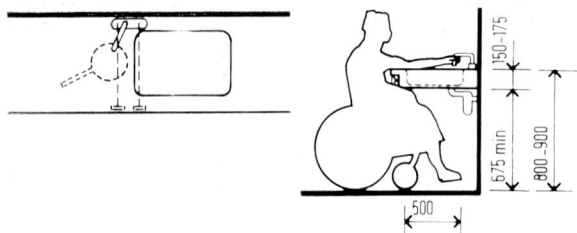

Kitchen fittings designed to suit disabled people; lowered worktops and shelves; sink with knee-space below; lever tap controls at front of worktop with swivel spout; large toe recess; bin-store, accessible from outside the dwelling, with hopper in worktop immediately to the right of the cooker.

be windows over the sink or worktops that the window ironmongery, curtains and blinds etc are easy to reach and to operate, especially for wheelchair users. Remote control winding mechanisms may also be required in this situation. The winding handle may be located conveniently just below worktop level at one side of the knee recess. (See 5.4.5).

5.6.13. Extract fans should preferably be operated by a switch within easy reach of a disabled person. (See 5.9.2). Pull-cord operated types should have cords sufficiently long to be readily accessible

5.7 BATHROOM AND WC

5.7.1. A major drawback for disabled people living in existing housing is that the bathroom is too small in floor area. Many of the problems of ambulant disabled people as well as wheelchair users could have been overcome simply by providing a wider door and sufficient space to turn their wheelchair or walking aid. As a rough guide, provided that there is a 900mm wide

doorset (see 5.3.2) and the bathroom layout permits a clear turning circle of 1500mm diameter (see 5.4.3) there will be sufficient space. Equally, if there is enough room to turn a wheelchair there will generally be adequate space for access to and use of the individual appliances.

5.7.2. Care should be taken in the planning of dwellings and the selection of house types to avoid those which strongly favour either left-handed or right-handed occupiers. This is particularly relevant in situations where, for instance, someone who is paralysed down one side might have great difficulty in using a bathroom which was the wrong way round because of the direction of approach to the bath or WC and the position of taps or grabrails. Where possible, alternative handed versions of each house type should be provided within a particular locality.

5.7.3. The design and layout of the bathroom should allow for flexibility in the precise choice and location of

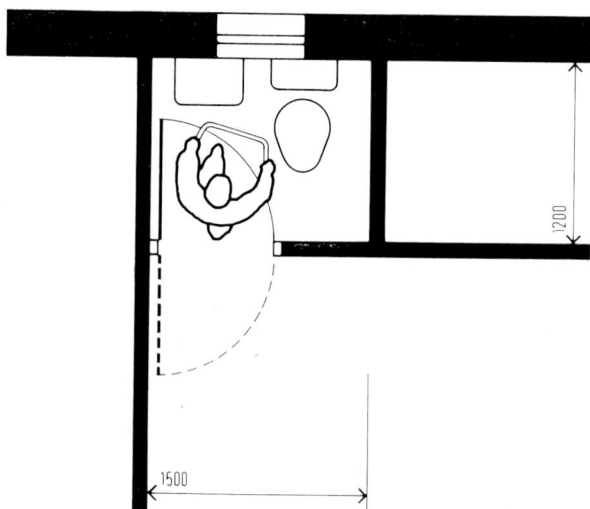

typical w.c. compartment which may be made suitable for ambulant disabled by providing an outward opening door

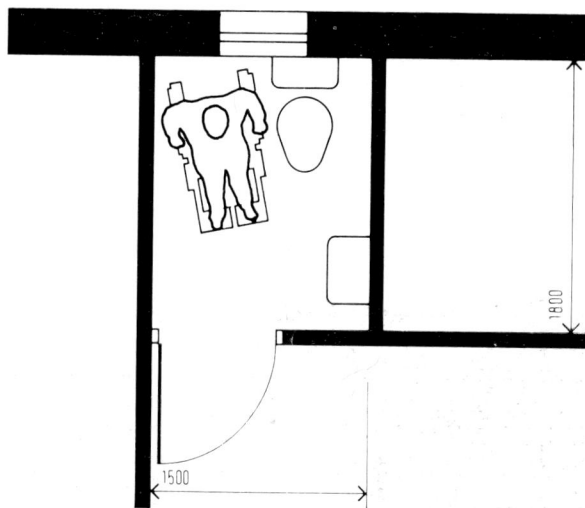

similar w.c. for wheelchair access requires a large increase in area

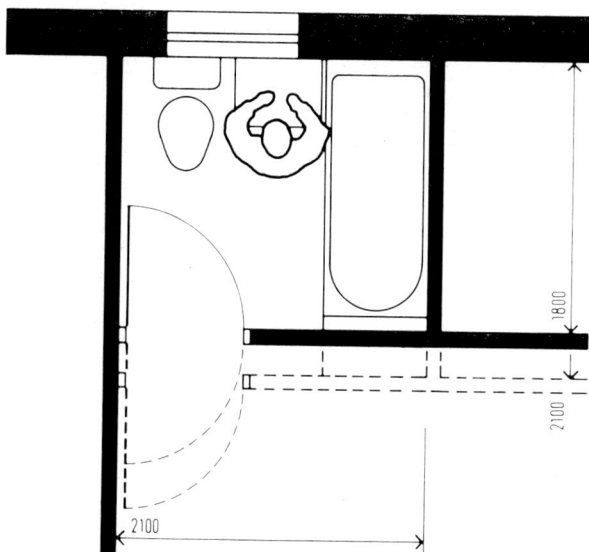

example of a standard bathroom layout which can readily be amended to suit ambulant disabled occupier (dotted line)

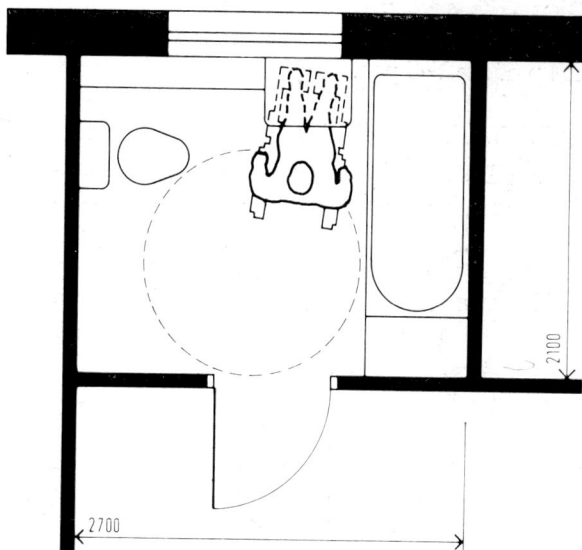

the equivalent bathroom in a wheelchair house enlarged to provide space for full wheelchair use

fixtures to suit individual requirements. In most small dwellings the WC fitting will be included in the bathroom and this is economical in terms of space provision as the wheelchair utilisation space for bath, basin and WC fitting can then overlap. However, severely disabled people may take a long time to use the WC or to wash themselves and this can become a source of friction in large households where other members may have to wait to use the bathroom. It is therefore recommended that in four person or larger dwellings designed to wheelchair standards a second WC with basin should be provided. Provision of bathrooms and WCs in ambulant disabled housing should be the same as for general needs housing standards except that there must always be at least a WC with basin at entrance level in two-storey dwellings. (See 5.3.8.)

5.7.4. Location of the fittings in the bathroom is very important and there should be sufficient space around the WC fitting to permit frontal or lateral wheelchair approach with room for someone to assist if needed. Generally, the activity space required, whether in a separate compartment or within a bathroom will be not less than 1500 × 1800mm with the centre-line of the fitting located 450mm away from one corner along the short side. A WC pan of standard height should be used and any increase in height which may be required can be achieved by using adjustable seat extensions or portable aids with adjustable legs and incorporating a seat and handrails. It is most important that the seat and its fixings are robust. If floor-standing WC pans are chosen, these should not have projecting plinths. Ideally, wall-mounted WC pans should be used to permit close access by wheelchairs. If low level cisterns are recessed they should be concealed behind a duct cover stout enough to support a grabrail behind the WC fitting. The flush handle should be located away from the side wall and should not be more than 1200mm above floor level. Toilet paper holders for interleaved paper in packs are preferable to rolls because they are easier to use with one hand. Paper holders should be positioned for easy reach by a person seated on the WC fitting. The suggested location is on the side wall 600-700mm above floor level and 300mm in front of the lip of the WC pan.

5.7.5. Wash-hand basins may project into the utilisation space for the WC fitting provided that they are cantilevered out from the wall without legs or other

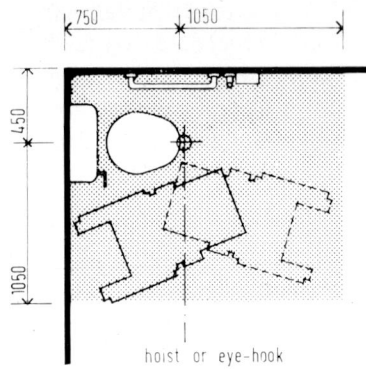

hoist or eye-hook

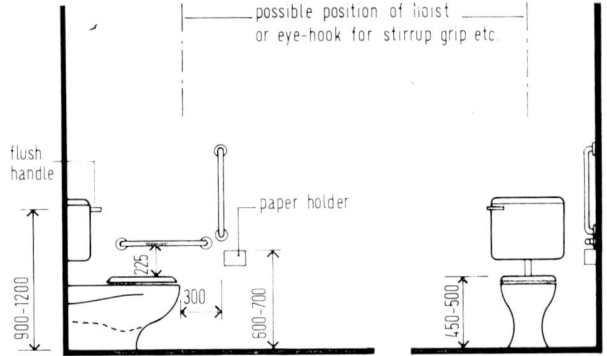

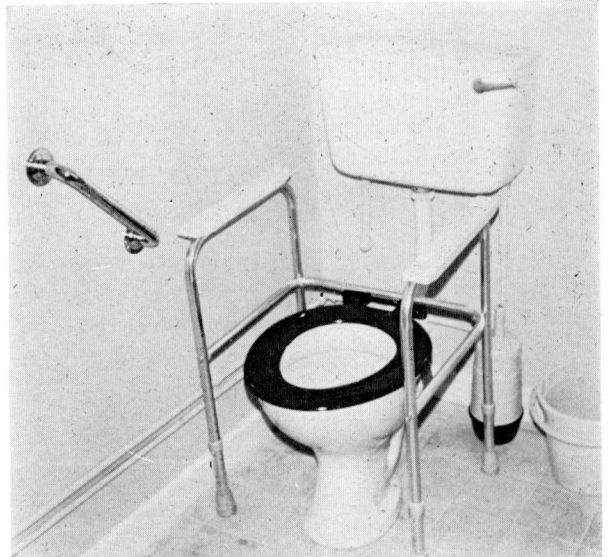

Additional grabrails at the WC provided by means of portable frame, adjustable for height.

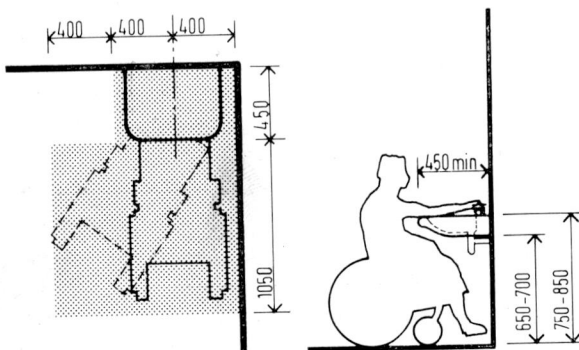

Basin set in tiled worktop with clear knee-space below; lever taps.

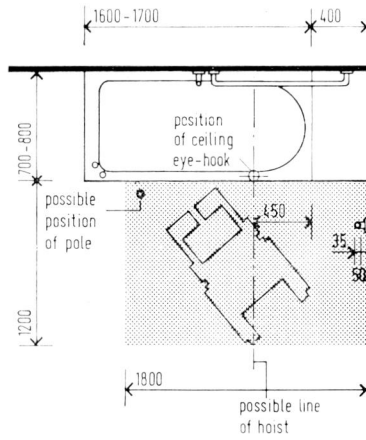

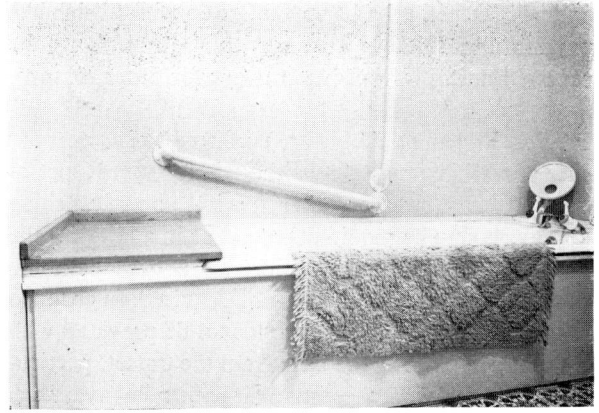

Bath with seat at head; thickening of bath roll to provide edge for gripping; robust grabrails with large flanges, for secure wall fixing; lever taps.

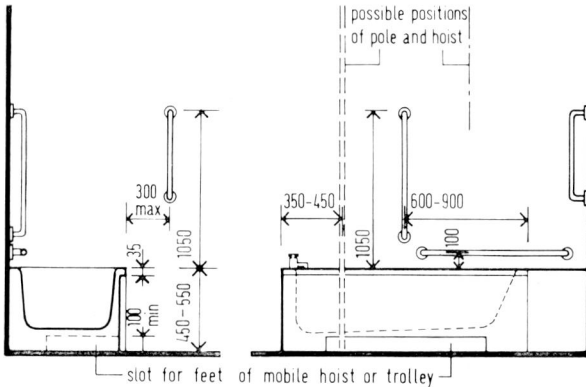

obstructions underneath. The clear space required for access to and use of the basin is about 1200 × 1500mm with the centre-line of the basin located 400mm from one corner along the short side. It is desirable that the basin should be set in a worktop and that this should be adjustable in height between 750mm for wheelchair users and 85mm for ambulant disabled people. (See 5.6.9). If possible, the fittings should be arranged so that the basin can be reached by a person seated on the WC fitting in order to facilitate hand washing after use of the WC, but this may be difficult to achieve in practice because of the space required for approach to the WC fitting. The edge of the basin or worktop should project at least 450mm to permit a wheelchair user to position himself sufficiently close to the basin. Any exposed hot water pipes should be covered or lagged to avoid scalding. (See 5.6.9).

5.7.6. A clear space of 1800 × 1200mm should be provided alongside the bath for access and assistance. The bath itself is normally 1600-1700mm long, 700-800mm wide and about 375mm deep with a flat bottomed profile. The rim of the bath should generally be 450mm above floor level although a higher bath rim at 500-550mm may be preferred in some cases. A deep recess or slot should be provided under the side of the bath to facilitate access for wheelchairs and mobile trolley hoists. Floor mounted hoists are also sometimes used at the edge of the bath. There must in all cases be a 400mm wide platform at the head of the bath to aid transfer from a wheelchair. The bath itself should be of solid construction the roll edges being used for support when getting in and out. Handles set into the bath roll

Use of seat at head of bath together with additional seat wedged between bath sides; note position of hands and use of grabrail and bathroll; corner position of taps for easy access; clear space beside bath for lateral approach.

can be helpful but must not project above the rim. Portable bath seats may be used in addition and these are usually wedged between the sides of the bath, or rely upon support from the rim on both sides of the bath. For this reason, acrylic baths should be avoided as they are liable not only to be damaged by the seats but can provide difficulty in sealing at wall junctions where there is continual movement with the weight of adults using the bath. The shiny surface on some new baths can be hazardous for the disabled; baths should be chosen with this aspect in mind, and in the context of adaptations it should be remembered that worn enamelled metal baths are often preferred by the tenants and suitable existing fittings should not be renewed unless obviously necessary for other reasons.

5.7.7. In general, baths are preferred to showers for ease of washing and safety although, for some types of disability a shower or other special type of washing appliance may be required instead or in addition. The normal provision will therefore be a bath with the possibility of installing a shower if required. In grouped schemes some of the dwellings could be provided with a shower in place of the bath from the outset, particularly if there was a communal bathroom available. Simple shower equipment can be fitted in conjunction with a bath so that a disabled person can take a shower while seated on the bath seat. In the adaptation of existing houses for use by disabled people, it may be desirable to install a shower in place of a bath in order to provide more manoeuvring space, if the existing bathroom is small and it is not feasible to enlarge it or to convert some other room.

5.7.8. Shower trays having a kerb or plinth may be awkward for disabled people although there are some types of tray which have one side lowered to facilitate access. Alternatively, the whole bathroom floor could be tanked and laid to fall to a floor gulley positioned close to the shower. Relaxation from the Building Regulations which require a kerb of 90mm, should be sought in respect of this facility, in order that a flush threshold may be retained at the bathroom door. In all bathrooms and WCs slippery floor finishes should be avoided.

5.7.9. The plumbing layout should be suitable for possible shower installations with the cold water storage tank positioned high enough to provide adequate water pressure.

5.7.10. The space allocated for the shower should be 1050mm wide × 900mm deep with a wheelchair utilisation space of 1200 × 1300mm in front of the shower. Where shower chairs may be used by severely disabled people the cubicle should be increased to 1200 × 1200mm thus permitting the chair to be wheeled completely into the cubicle. Shower cubicles should be provided with a hinged seat or bench 350mm deep set at a height of 450mm along the approach side of the cubicle. The shower rose should be fitted with a flexible hose and have a variety of alternative head positions on the back wall of the cubicle up to a height of 1900mm above floor level. The shower head may also be clamped to a pole in order to provide vertical adjustment. The shower control valves and a recessed soap and sponge tray should be located within easy reach of a person sitting on the seat, at a height of about 1050mm.

5.7.11. It is essential for thermostatic temperature controls to be fitted to hot water supplies to showers in disabled persons' dwellings because of the danger of scalding for those with sensory impairment.

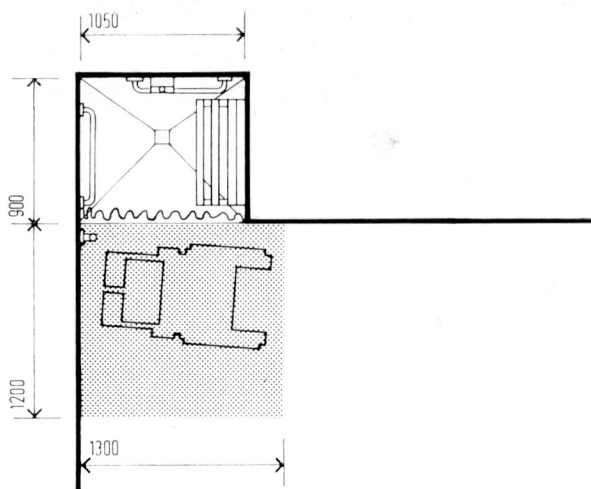

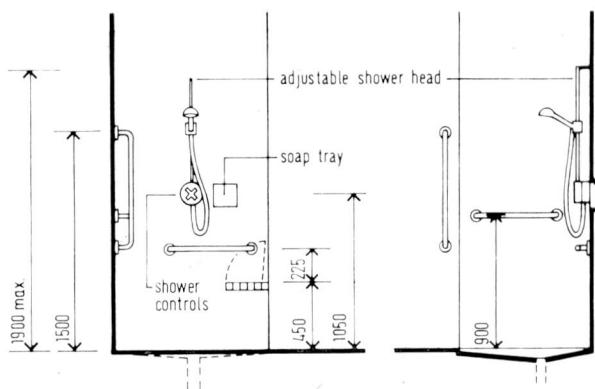

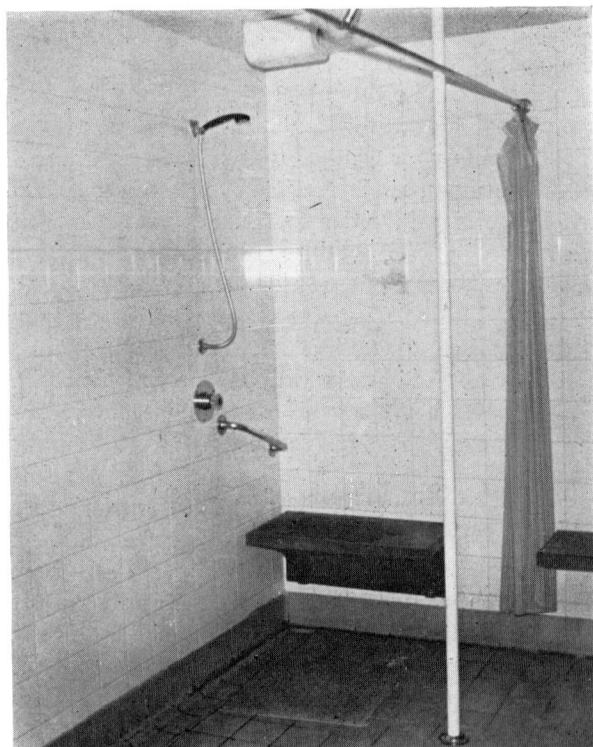

Shower (communal bathroom in sheltered housing scheme); seats inside and outside; stout grabrail and pole; floor level to fall to drainage channel.

5.7.12. Taps should be selected for easy manipulation, metal capstan types being preferred. Lever taps are desirable if the occupier has specific manipulatory

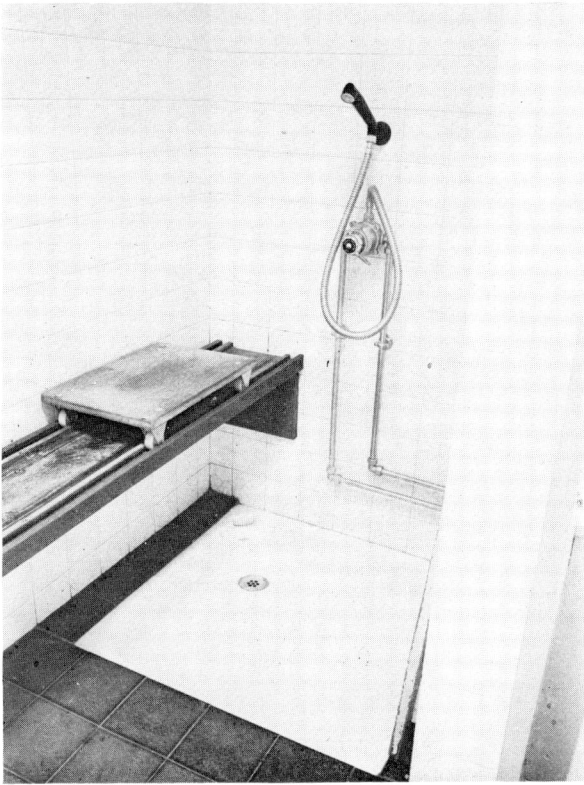

Shower with ingenious seat on rollers, handheld shower head; mixer valve is essential but exposed hot pipe could be a hazard.

Shallow bath insert to reduce amount of bending required of an assistant bathing a disabled person.

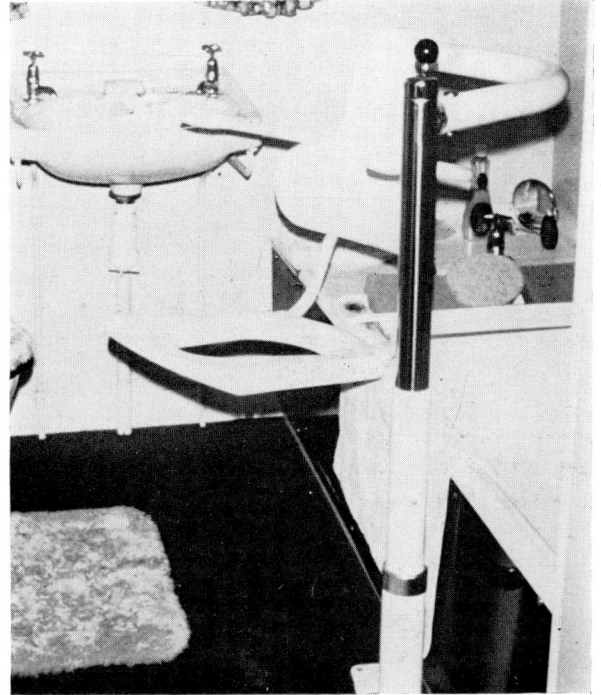

Floor-mounted bath hoist; seat swivels over edge of bath and is raised or lowered by winding handle on top.

Wheeled shower chair; bathroom floor dished to outlet gulley; adjustable shower fitting and mixer valves with concealed pipe, too high for convenient use by seated person.

Moulded glass-fibre seat placed over WC fitting, providing extra support for disabled person.

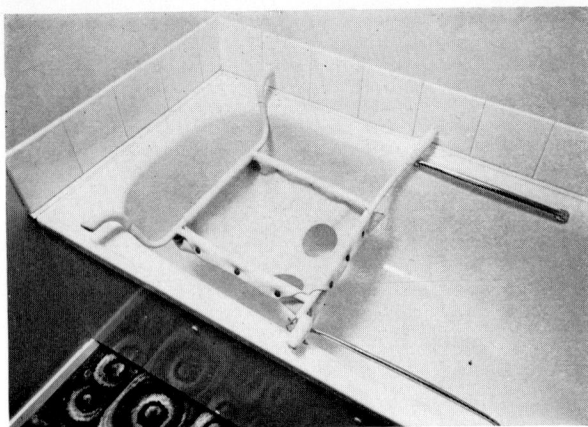

Bathing aid for use by small disabled child.

Bathroom layout providing space for wheelchair manoeuvre; basin suitable for seated hair-washing; lever taps; robust grabrails around WC fitting to facilitate frontal or lateral wheelchair approach as well as movement between WC and basin; raised seat; note use of high-level cistern to provide space for grabrails but chain-pull much too short—out of picture and out of reach.

disabilities or has difficulty reaching conventional taps. Some types of grabrails for use at the bath are intended to be clamped onto the taps, which should therefore be sufficiently robust and suitably designed for that purpose. Cylindrical taps should be avoided.

5.7.13. There is a wide variety of grabrails and handles available for use in the bathroom and WC. Selection and positioning of these should be left where possible until the individual requirements of a particular occupier can be established. Where an occupier is known in advance, the advice of an occupational therapist should be sought and close liaison should be maintained with the local authority social work department concerning installation of any special equipment. It is essential that walls of bathrooms and WCs should be suitable for fixing grabrails capable of supporting the weight of a person; some types of lightweight hollow partitions would be unsuitable for this purpose. Examples of grabrails generally suitable for most disabled people are a horizontal rail and a vertical rail on the side wall over the bath, a vertical rail on the wall beside the seat at the head of the bath, vertical and horizontal rails on the wall beside the WC fitting, a horizontal rail below the shower fitting, and a vertical rail beside the shower seat. (See diagrams). It should also be remembered that other fixtures are frequently used for steadying or for support, especially basins, and the fixings need to be carefully designed accordingly.

5.7.14. In wheelchair housing ceilings should be of suitable construction to permit the installation where needed of vertical poles, chain and stirrup grips, hoists and track. Bolts should be fixed through the ceiling structure at key locations, with the threaded end projecting below the ceiling finish and protected with a washer and closed hexagonal nut, to permit subsequent fixing of eye-bolts or ceiling beams. Bolts should be located above the edge of the bath, the lip of the WC fitting, and the entrance to the shower cubicle. (See diagrams). They should also be located along the line of a possible hoist track between the WC fitting and the bath, passing above the wheelchair manoeuvring space. Similar provision may be made in bedrooms in anticipation of a ceiling mounted hoist being used for transferring a severely disabled person from the bed to wheelchair or commode. (See 5.5.4). In some layouts it may be possible to arrange for the bathroom to open directly off the bedroom so that a ceiling hoist and track can be provided directly between bed, WC and bath. This facility could readily be obtained in the design of one and two person dwellings although in larger dwellings it would require the introduction of a second bathroom. Relaxation of the Building Standards (Scotland) Regulations, which require that WCs/bathrooms should be separated from habitable apartments by a ventilated lobby, should be sought in respect of this item.

5.7.15. Door locks in bathrooms and WCs should be chosen to enable the doors to be opened from outside in the event of an emergency; side-hung doors should open outwards in case a frail or disabled person collapses or falls against the inside of the door. (See 5.3.6, 5.4.4-5).

5.8 STORAGE FACILITIES

5.8.1. In conventional general needs dwelling design the bulk of general storage is often provided in one large space in order to meet statutory nett space requirements, and other storage provisions are normally concentrated in spaces having a vertical emphasis such as cupboards, wardrobes and book-cases. In designing for the disabled, however, where shelf usability and access is paramount, narrow, deep, built-in cupboards and very high or very low shelves will generally be inaccessible and long horizontal shelves or shallow wall-mounted units, within living or circulation areas, are considered to be more suitable. However, bulk general storage and some high level cupboards would still be required for storage of large or infrequently used items such as trunks or luggage which could be reached by a helper or another member of the family when needed.

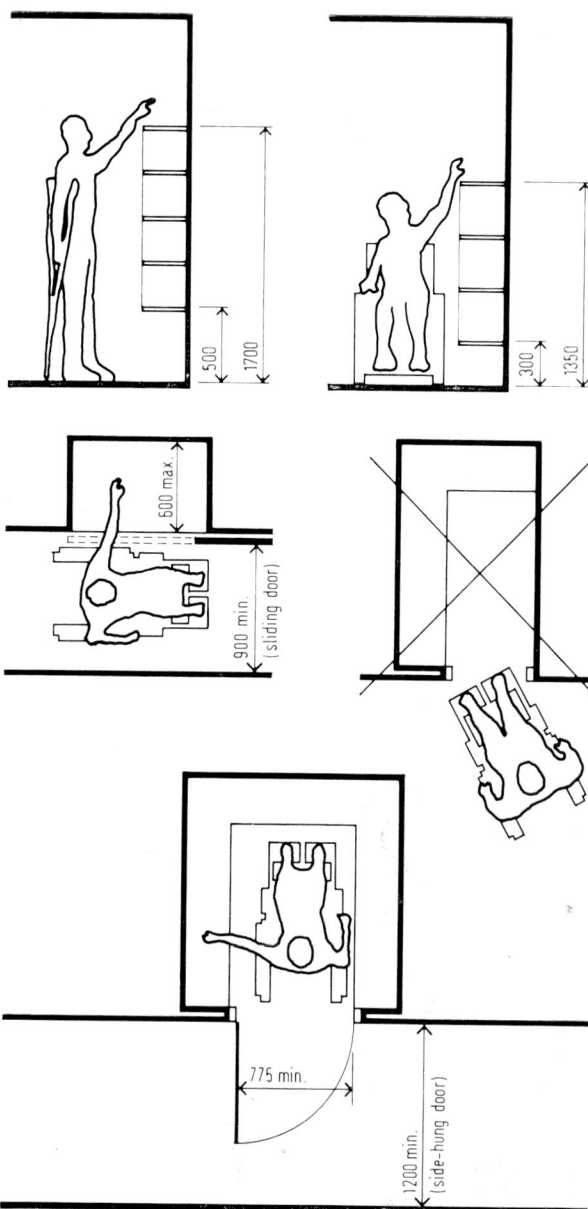

5.8.2. The most suitable zone for location of storage shelves for access by ambulant disabled people is between 500mm and 1700mm above floor level. The equivalent zone for wheelchair users is 300mm to 1350mm respectively. Where the disabled person has to reach across an obstruction such as a kitchen worktop the upper limit is reduced to 1600mm for ambulant disabled and 1250mm for wheelchair users. (See 5.6.3).

5.8.3. Drawers should be well fitting and easy to slide and should be provided with a stop to prevent complete withdrawal. They are most accessible when located between about 450mm and 900mm above floor level. Each drawer should preferably be shallow for ease of access and a depth of 150mm is suggested as a maximum. A single central handle rather than two handles is essential for one-handed users or those needing to use one hand for body support. Handles for drawers and cupboard doors should provide a full hand grip, such as may be achieved by using tubular D-handles or cut out slots. Rim or edge finger grips

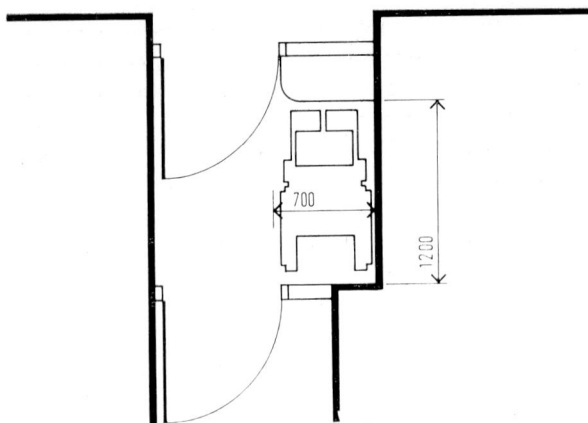

are unsuitable as they can be awkward for those with a manipulatory disability.

5.8.4. Where large built-in cupboards are used they should be designed as rooms with 900mm wide door-sets arranged to permit a person using a wheelchair or walking aid to enter forwards and reverse out. Narrower doors may be accessible for some wheelchairs but it should be remembered that at the point when the wheelchair starts to reverse the small front wheels swivel round on their vertical axes and can cause the wheelchair to jam in the doorway or at least inflict damage upon the woodwork. Sliding doors are preferred for small cupboards so as not to intrude into the circulation space but they can be awkward for disabled people to use. (See 5.3.5). Accessibility to wardrobe alcoves can be improved by using curtains across the opening rather than doors. (See 5.5.3).

5.8.5. In wheelchair housing there is also the problem of storing wheelchairs, mobile hoists and other equipment. Special cupboards may not be easily accessible for this purpose and open alcoves or generous space allowances within living and circulation areas are preferred for temporary parking of such items. In some dwellings a spare bedroom may be used for this purpose. The space required for wheelchair storage is approximately 1200 × 700mm. However in family dwellings a storage space of about 1800 × 700mm should be allowed in order to accommodate a pram as well as a wheelchair. The use of an enclosed porch or entrance lobby may be appropriate, and space should also be provided in association with a garage or carport for temporary wheelchair storage.

5.9 SERVICES AND FITTINGS

5.9.1. In ambulant disabled housing the heating system will normally be designed to the same standards as for general needs housing. However, where the occupier is elderly, and may suffer from poor blood circulation, a higher performance is recommended. In wheelchair housing there should be a space heating installation capable of maintaining a temperature of 21°C in all rooms when the outside temperature is −1°C. Where practicable the temperature level should be individually controllable in each room. Heating appliances should be selected for fire safety as well as ease of operation, with thermostats or control switches readily accessible, preferably between 600mm and 1200mm above floor level. The attention of services consultants should be drawn to the need for care in the choice and location of radiators, storage heaters and other appliances so as not to intrude into circulation spaces. (See 5.2.2).

5.9.2. It is particularly important to provide adequate lighting levels in housing for the disabled because of the difficulty which occupiers may have in taking work to the light or in holding reading material in a suitable position. Elderly disabled people may also be suffering some impairment of vision and artificial lighting installations should therefore be designed to be capable of achieving a reasonable standard of illumination and a good general distribution of light source. Light switches should be of straightforward design and simple positive action and should be located so as to align with the door handles, normally between 900mm and 1050mm above floor levels. Cord operated light switches should have large distinctive knobs or handles.

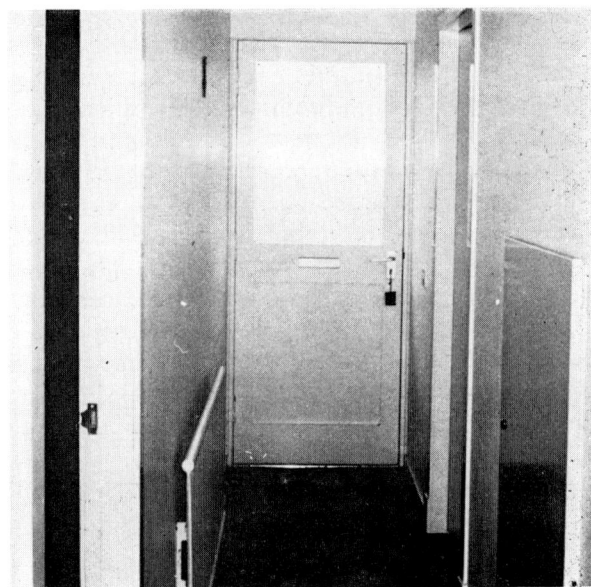

Narrow entrance hall, aggravated by location of radiator.

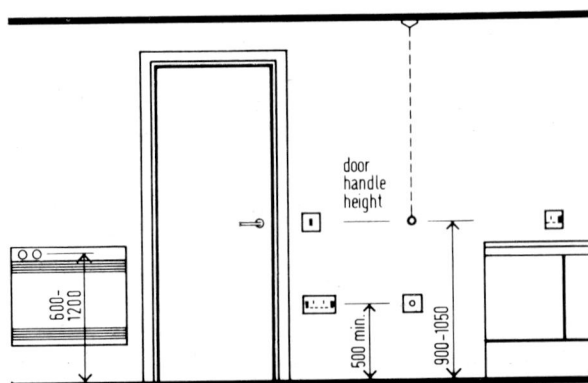

5.9.3. Power outlet, telephone and TV aerial sockets should be located at a height of not less than 500mm above floor level. In some parts of the dwelling it may be desirable to position these at door handle height, especially where furniture is likely to be placed nearby, for instance in kitchens, where the sockets should be above worktop level. However, high level sockets can sometimes present a hazard because of trailing flexes and should therefore be used with caution. Shaver sockets should be located between 900mm and 1200mm above floor level, so that they may be used from a seated position, rather than in the light fitting above a mirror where they may be inaccessible.

5.9.4. Electricity and gas meters, fuse boxes, main switches, valves, taps and water stop-cocks should be placed within reach of a disabled person and should not be housed in deep narrow cupboards or at very high or low levels. Positioning of meters so that they may be inspected from outside the dwelling through a glass panel beside the entrance door is a desirable feature as it permits meter reading without having to disturb a disabled or elderly tenant.

5.9.5. In sheltered housing schemes for disabled people, a call system is connected to the warden's dwelling or office, where there is a switch board indicating the origin of the call. These systems are actuated from within the dwelling by clearly identifiable bell-pushes or cord-pulls set in strategic positions in every room. Cord-pulls should reach down to floor level to permit operation from a prone position in case the disabled person falls and, they should be located away from any cord operated light switch in the same room and they should be distinctively coloured. In bathrooms, cords should be reachable from the bath. Cancellation switches are generally located near to the entrance door of each dwelling. (See Scottish Housing Handbook, Part 5: 'Housing for the Elderly' for further details of installation and use). It is desirable that housing for the disabled should be considered with the provision of statutory or voluntary local centres, health centres or day clubs, which the disabled occupiers can call upon for assistance in an emergency either by using an alarm system or simply by telephone (see 5.10.7), and this can effectively combine the advantages of independent dwellings with at least some of the security of sheltered housing. (See 4.1.4, 4.2.1).

5.9.6. Entrance door bells with intercoms or door answering devices may be a desirable feature for an elderly or disabled person confined to bed or chair-bound, particularly in flatted accommodation. Door bells can also be connected to flashing light systems to cater for the deaf or hard of hearing. These should be designed so as to remain in operation after release of the bell-push until cancellation by the occupier.

5.9.7. There is now a wide range of special equipment and aids which may be helpful for particular handicapped people. Advice should be sought from an occupational therapist or other person qualified to make an assessment of the suitability of various items of equipment in individual cases. Information concerning specific items of equipment may also be obtained from the Scottish Information Service for the Disabled, 18/19 Claremont Crescent, Edinburgh EH7 4QD.

5.10 TENANTS FURNISHINGS AND EQUIPMENT

5.10.1. This section contains advice on certain items which would not be the responsibility of the housing authority but would be provided by the occupier of the dwelling.

5.10.2. Curtains should be cord operated, with a continuous loop so that the ends of the cord do not rise out of reach when the curtain is in an extreme

Adjustable height table/desk for disabled person.

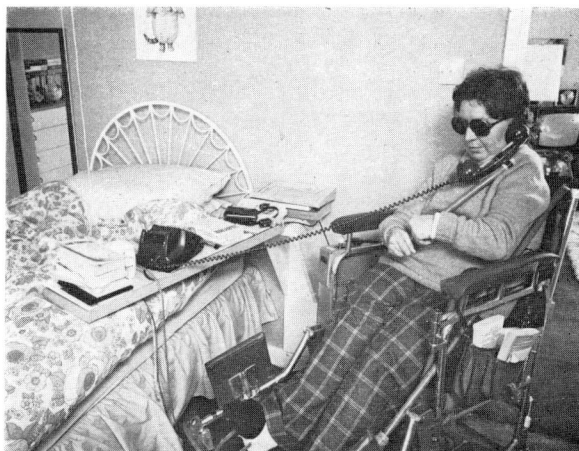

Swivelling bedside shelf wall-mounted; telephone handset extension facilitates use by person with limited arm mobility.

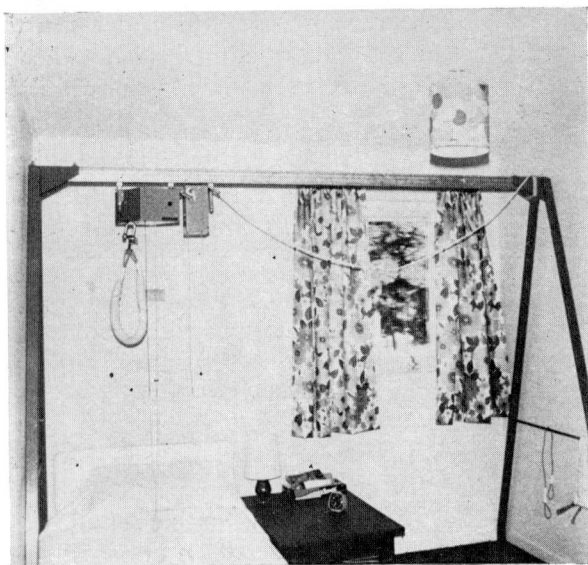

Where walls and ceiling are unsuitable, gantry is used to mount hoist and track over bed and circulation space.

with those of the ambulant with regard to height of tables and worktops. In order to provide adequate knee space for the ambulant the clear height underneath the table should be 670mm with the top surface at approximately 700-750mm. However, for wheelchair access the table should ideally be about 100mm higher, which would be unsuitable for normal use by other people. In practice, a table of normal height will be installed in family dwellings where there is likely to be this conflict, and the meal of a wheelchair user who has difficulty eating from that height will probably be taken from a tray or an adjustable cantilever trolley. Wheelchair users may also remove armrests to gain access to low tables or worktops. (See 5.1.6).

position. Removal of curtains, upholstery and other furnishings for cleaning could undoubtedly be made easier by careful selection of fittings and fastenings, but it is more likely that in practice these kinds of occasional tasks would be carried out by someone other than the disabled persons themselves.

5.10.7. For many disabled people, who may be unable to go out much or who live alone, the telephone can be a great boon providing an essential link with the outside world. Local authority social work departments may be able to assist with telephone installation or retention in some cases. Installation of a push-button telephone in place of the conventional dialling apparatus can be particularly useful for those with a manipulatory handicap. Additional security may be given to severely disabled people if there is a local contact point which they may call by telephone for assistance in an emergency. (See 5.9.5).

5.10.3. Opinions vary widely over which type of floor finish is appropriate for the handicapped but tenants will in practice almost certainly wish to have a carpet in the living room and bedrooms. In general, firm even surfaces are most suitable for wheelchairs, while carpets are preferable for ambulant disabled people and others liable to accidental falls. A suggested compromise suitable for general application in living areas might be fitted carpets with short pile and non-resilient non-slip backings. Where possible carpets should be securely fixed at the edges to avoid curling or rucking. Any kind of loose rugs or matting can present a serious safety hazard to disabled people.

BIBLIOGRAPHY

Designing for the Disabled, 3rd Edition, Goldsmith, Royal Institute of British Architects, London 1976.

Housing for Old People with Design Standards for the Disabled, New Scottish Housing Handbook Bulletin 3 SDD, HMSO 1970.

Access for the Disabled to Buildings, Part 2: Housing Design: Convenience for Disabled People, BSCP96 British Standards Institute, London 1976. (Draft).

A Handbook of Housing for Disabled People, Penton and Barlow, London Housing Consortium, West Group, 1976.

Housing for Disabled People, Sharp, Eric Cole Design Group, Cirencester 1974.

Housing for the Disabled, Planning Digest, Scottish Local Authorities Special Housing Group, Edinburgh 1972.

Housing for Special Needs, Part 1: The Physically Handicapped, Scottish Local Authorities Special Housing Group, Edinburgh 1974.

An Introduction to Domestic Design for the Disabled, Walter, Disabled Living Foundation, London 1969.

Four Architectural Movement Studies for the Wheelchair and Ambulant Disabled, Walter, Disabled Living Foundation, London 1971.

Safety in the Home, MOHLG, Design Bulletin 13, Acland, HMSO, London 1967.

A J Metric Handbook, 3rd Edition, Fairweather and Sliwa, The Architectural Press, London 1970.

5.10.4. For some types of disability where incontinence is a problem it is desirable that floor finishes and upholstery materials should be easy to clean, and in such cases carpets or covers which can be readily removed may be advantageous, particularly in the bedroom. Floor finishes, curtains and upholstery should also be chosen with fire safety in mind as some synthetic materials are likely to be unsatisfactory in situations where disabled tenants may be accident prone.

5.10.5. The use of lightweight continental quilts can greatly facilitate bed-making particularly in the smaller bedrooms where a disabled person might have difficulty in reaching both sides of the bed to tuck in conventional sheets and blankets.

5.10.6. Standard dining chairs and tables will generally be satisfactory for the ambulant disabled, but the requirements of a wheelchair user may conflict

5.1 *Metric Space Standards*, New Scottish Housing Handbook Bulletin 1, SDD, HMSO 1968.

5.1 *A Guide to User Activity Measurements in Health Buildings*, DHSS Design Note 3, HMSO 1969.

5.3 *Wheelchair Housing: A Survey of Purpose-Designed Dwellings for Disabled People*, Morton, Housing Development Directorate, DOE 1976.

5.3 *Wheelchair Housing*, Midland Housing Consortium, Coventry 1976.

5.6 *A Pilot Study of Disabled Housewives in their Kitchens*, Howie, Central Council for the Disabled, London 1968.

5.6 *Disabled Housewives in their Kitchens*, Disabled Living Foundation, London 1969.

5.6 *Spaces in the Home: Kitchens and Laundering Spaces*, DOE Design Bulletin 24, Part 2, HMSO 1972.

5.7 *Spaces in the Home: Bathrooms and WCs*, DOE Design Bulletin 24, Part 1, HMSO 1972.

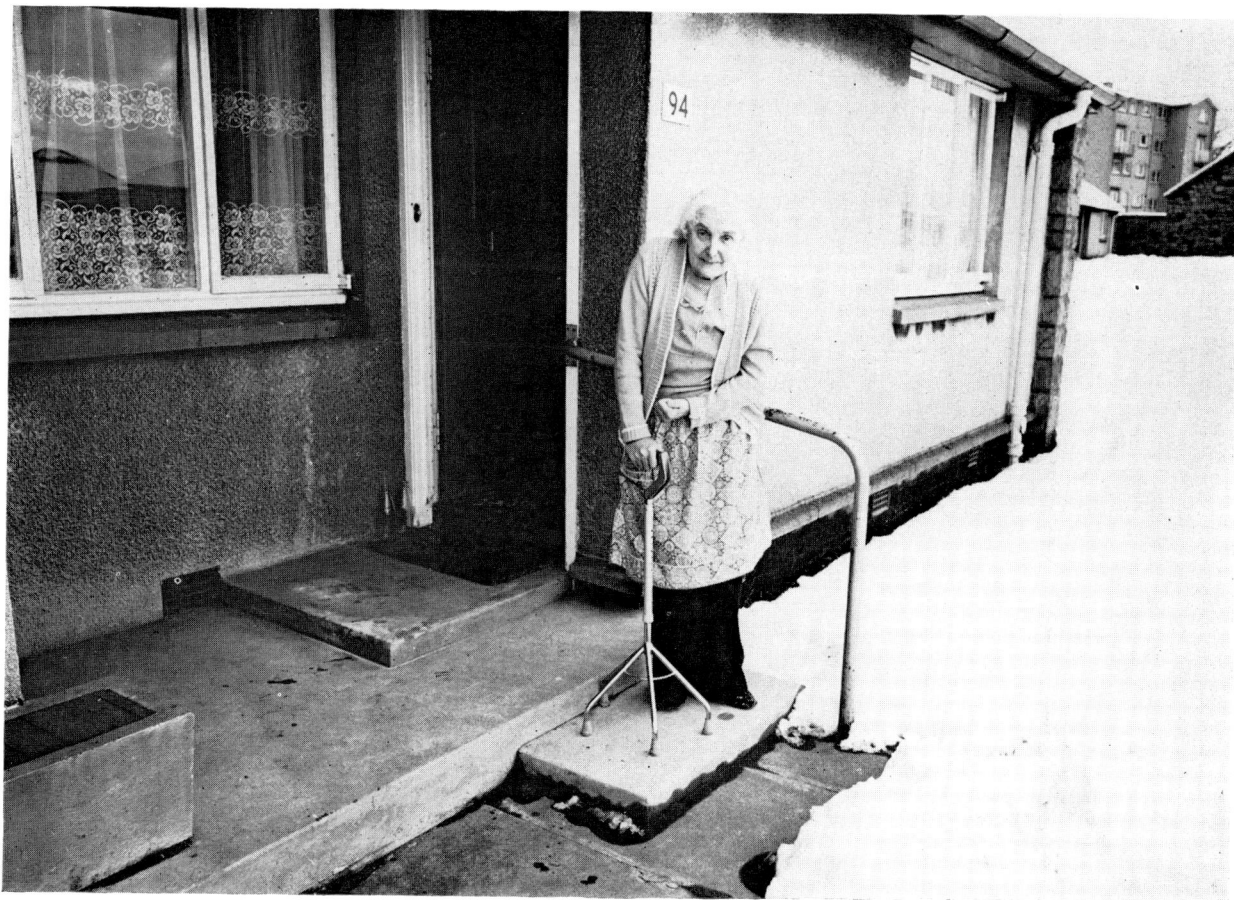

Housing for the Disabled

6.1 APPLICATION OF STANDARDS

6.1.1. The lists of features contained in this section are intended to act as a checklist of those items which should be incorporated into the design of dwellings in order to create ambulant disabled housing or wheelchair housing, irrespective of whether these are newly built or adaptations to existing buildings.

6.1.2. The items described as essential are intended to cover the main features required to define the type of dwelling, but the lists are not exhaustive. Examples of additional features, which could with advantage be selected to suit particular circumstances, are listed as optional items for each type of dwelling.

6.1.3. The standards contained in 6.2 *Ambulant Disabled Housing* and in 6.3 *Wheelchair Housing* are confined to those which relate to the structure of the dwellings and the design of fittings and equipment insofar as the special requirements of the disabled affect items which would normally be provided by a housing authority in mainstream housing. There are many other special types of equipment or aids to daily living which might be beneficial to particular disabled tenants and these usually will be the responsibility of health boards or local authority social work departments rather than the housing authority.

6.2 AMBULANT DISABLED HOUSING

6.2.1. The design of ambulant disabled housing is based upon the space and amenity standards for mainstream dwellings with the addition of the features listed below. These items are essential for ordinary housing to achieve ambulant disabled housing standards and details of the design are discussed more fully in the preceding sections.

1. Level or ramped approach for access purposes to be at least 1200mm wide with gradient not exeeding 1:12 and preferably 1:20. (4.3.3-9).
2. Ambulant disabled housing in flats must be accessible without climbing stairs. Lifts must have doors giving at least 800mm clear opening width. There must also be suitably designed fire escape stairs to places of safety. (4.4.6-9).
3. Two-storey dwellings would be acceptable provided that there is at least a WC with WHB at entrance level and a straight flight staircase to facilitate installation of a chairlift, and that one of the ground floor rooms is usable as a bedroom for the disabled member of the household. (5.3.8).
4. Circulation spaces to be at least 900mm wide throughout. (5.2.2, 5.3.1).
5. Doors to all rooms and entrance to give at least 775mm clear opening width (900mm doorset). (5.2.1, 5.3.2).
6. Thresholds at entrance doors preferably to be flush or not more than 20mm above the floor to

either side. Internal doors to have flush thresholds. (5.2.3, 5.3.3).
7. Walls in bathroom and WC to be suitable for fixing support rails. (5.7.13).

6.2.2. Incorporation of the following desirable features may also be considered in some circumstances; they should only be provided to cater for the identified needs of a particular disabled occupier.

1. Car parking space to be provided close to the dwelling. (4.5.1-2).
2. Garden paths, other than main dwelling access, to be at least 900mm wide. (4.6.2).
3. Door and window ironmongery to be selected for easy manipulation and located at appropriate levels for easy operation. (5.3.6, 5.4.5).
4. Living room windows to be designed for seated person to see outside view. (5.4.4, 5.5.5).
5. Worktops and storage units/shelves to be adjustable for height. (5.6.3-6, 5.8.1-2).
6. Swivel spout to kitchen sink taps to be offset for kettle filling with taps selected for easy manipulation. (5.6.10).
7. Flooring materials in kitchen, bathroom and WC to be non-slip. (5.6.11, 5.7.8).
8. Seat 400mm wide to be provided at head of bath. (5.7.6).
9. Basic support rails to be fitted in bathroom and WC. (5.7.13).
10. Light switches to have controls easy to operate and located at door handle height, 900-1050 mm above floor level. (5.9.2).
11. Power sockets to be situated at a minimum height of 500mm above floor level. (5.9.3).
12. Heating controls, meters, main switches and fuse boxes to be located for easy reach. (5.9.1).

6.3 WHEELCHAIR HOUSING

6.3.1. The following items are essential for wheelchair housing standards to be achieved.

1. Level or ramped approach for access to be at least 1200mm wide and of a suitable gradient. (4.3.3-9).
2. Wheelchair housing should be designed as single storey dwellings at ground level. However, in certain circumstances, a two-storey dwelling design can be adapted for use as a wheelchair house if the bathroom and bedroom used by the disabled person are at entrance level. (4.4.10, 5.3.8).
3. Carport to be provided with undercover access to dwelling minimum clear space 5700 × 3300 mm. (4.5.3-6).
4. Garden paths, other than main dwelling access, to be at least 900mm wide. (4.6.2).
5. Enhanced space standards as set out in 5.1. (5.1.3).
6. Additional space for manoeuvring wheelchair to be provided in all main rooms (living, dining, kitchen, bathroom and at least the handicapped person's bedroom). (5.1.3, 5.3.1).

7. Additional WC and wash hand basin to be provided in single storey four person and larger dwellings. (5.3.8).

8. Entrance hall width to be 1200mm minimum with 300mm clear space at opening side of entrance door. (5.2.2).

9. Doors to all rooms and entrance to give at least 775mm clear opening width (900mm doorset). (5.2.1, 5.3.2).

10. Thresholds at entrance doors preferably to be flush or not more than 20mm above the floor level to either side. Internal doors to have flush thresholds. (5.2.3, 5.3.3).

11. Internal mailbasket and deliveries shelf to be provided beside front door. (5.2.6).

12. Doors to be hung to suit wheelchair user with hinges towards nearest corners of rooms. (5.3.4-5).

13. Door and window ironmongery to be selected for easy manipulation and located at appropriate levels for easy operation. (5.3.6, 5.4.4-5).

14. Protection to be provided for salient angles of walls, or hard plaster specification. (4.4.5, 5.3.7).

15. Living room windows to be designed for seated person to see outside view. (5.4.4).

16. Height of worktops and storage units/shelves to be adjustable, with a knee recess. (5.6.3-6, 5.8.1-2).

17. Kitchen sink to have internal depth 125-150mm and to be adjustable in height 800-850mm, with knee recess at least 670mm high × 750mm wide × 500mm deep. (5.6.9).

18. Swivel spout to kitchen sink taps to be offset for kettle filling, with taps selected for easy manipulation. (5.6.10).

19. Flooring materials in kitchen, bathroom and WC to be non-slip. (5.6.11, 5.7.8).

20. WC fitting to be sited for lateral, oblique and frontal approach from a wheelchair. (5.7.4).

21. Wash hand basin to be set in a cantilevered worktop with unobstructed knee space underneath. (5.7.5).

22. Seat 400mm wide to be provided at head of bath, and bath to be provided with toe recess to facilitate access from a wheelchair or mobile hoist. (5.7.6).

23. Cold water tank to be located so as to provide sufficient head of water for possible shower installation. (5.7.9).

24. Walls in bathroom and WC to be suitable for fixing grabrails. (5.7.13).

25. Basic support rails to be fitted in bathroom and WC. (5.7.13).

26. Ceiling in bathroom, WC and the handicapped person's bedroom to be suitable for possible fixing of hoist or track with eye bolts and/or ceiling beam. (5.5.4, 5.7.14).

27. Space heating installation to be capable of maintaining a temperature of 21°C in all rooms when the outside temperature is -1°C. (5.9.1).

28. Light switches to have controls easy to operate and located at door handle height, 900-1050mm above floor level. (5.9.2).

29. Power sockets to be situated at a minimum height of 500mm above floor level. (5.9.3).

30. Heating controls, meters, main switches and fuse boxes to be located within easy reach for the wheelchair user. (5.9.4).

6.3.2. Incorporation of the following desirable features may also be considered in some circumstances; they should only be provided to cater for the identified needs of a particular disabled occupier.

1. Garage to be provided with pull light switch, cross beam for stirrup grip or hoist and power point for charger, and level access to dwelling. (4.5.5-6).

2. Rotating clothes dryer to be provided for each dwelling. (4.6.4).

3. Sliding doors to be provided in main rooms. (5.3.5).

4. Door to be fitted with kicking plates and protective edges. (5.3.7).

5. Living room to have bay window for view of outside from wheelchair. (5.4.4).

6. Built-in cupboards to be provided in bedroom, with sliding doors or curtains for wheelchair access, and adjustable height hanging rail 1500-1800mm above floor level. (5.5.3).

7. Special kitchen storage units to be 500mm deep, incorporating large toe recesses 300mm high × 180mm deep, with an overhanging worktop for grip support and pull-out working surfaces 670mm above floor level. (5.6.6).

8. Independent low level storage trolleys to be provided in kitchen. (5.6.6).

9. Additional support rails to be fitted in bathroom and WC. (5.7.13).

10. Bathroom to open off bedroom providing a direct route for hoist track between bed, bath and WC. (5.7.14).

11. Shower to be provided instead of or in addition to bath, with floor laid to fall to floor gulley. (5.7.7-11).

6.4 SPECIAL EQUIPMENT AND SERVICES

6.4.1. The provision of aids or equipment is the responsibility of the health board where

(i) they are directly related to the management of an illness, especially to facilitate the patient's domiciliary nursing care or to the rehabilitation of a patient from hospital eg supplying bedpans, air-ring cushions, etc, or

(ii) the skills of a particular discipline within the health service are appropriate to the prescription and use of aids required on medical grounds eg supplying sticks, crutches, walking frames, wheelchairs, mobile hoists, spectacles, hearing-aids, etc.

(iii) where the work involves installation of a renal dialysis unit together with any alterations or adaptations to houses to accommodate it.

6.4.2. The provision of aids or equipment is the responsibility of the social work department where they are required to help the disabled person achieve a greater independence within his own home and are predominantly of a domestic character eg provision of raised toilet seats, free-standing toilet support rails, removable bath rails, bath seats or boards, bath tap shower fittings, plugs with handles, telephone aids, special furniture and utensils, etc.

BIBLIOGRAPHY

6.1   *Wheelchair and Mobility Housing: Standards and Costs,* DOE Circular No 92/1975, Welsh Office Circular No 163/1975

6.2   *Mobility Housing,* DOE/HDD Occasional Paper 2/1974

6.3   *Wheelchair Housing,* DOE/HDD Occasional Paper 2/1975

6.4   *Provision by Health Boards and Local Authorities of Aids and Equipment for Disabled People Living at Home and Adaptations to their Homes,* SED/SWSG Circular No 19/1976

6.4   *Home Dialysis,* (Second Edition) Scottish Local Authorities Special Housing Group, Edinburgh 1978.

ACKNOWLEDGEMENTS

937B

The Scottish Development Department gratefully acknowledges assistance received in the preparation of this part of the Scottish Housing Handbook from a large number of sources, and for the co-operation of the Scottish Home and Health Department and the Social Work Services Group of the Scottish Education Department in contributing to the Working Party set up to study the housing needs of the disabled.

Much useful advice and information has also been received from housing associations, local authority housing and social work departments, occupational therapists, architects in local government and private practice, and many other interested organisations, professional groups and individuals. We are grateful to the various authors or editors who have kindly permitted us to make use of the detailed information contained in the many documents referred to in the bibliography. Special mention should also be made of the work in this field, published or unpublished, of the Housing Development Directorate of the Department of the Environment. We would also like to acknowledge the assistance received from Selwyn Goldsmith, MA (Cantab), author of "Designing for the Disabled".

In addition, we wish to record our gratitude to those disabled people who have permitted us to visit them in their homes and who have contributed many valuable comments and suggestions on the design and equipment of their dwellings.

Housing for the Disabled

logic with boolean Algebra